Peacemaking

Resolving Conflict, Restoring and Building Harmony in Relationships

DR. RICK LOVE

Peacemaking
Resolving Conflict, Restoring and Building Harmony in Relationships

A STUDY GUIDE

Peacemaking: A Study Guide
Resolving Conflict, Restoring & Building Harmony in Relationships
by Rick Love
Peacemaking Applied
by Elliot Paulson

Copyright © 2001 Rick Love

All rights reserved.

No part of this publication may be reproduced, stored in a retrieval system, or transmitted in any form or by any means — electroinic, mechanical, photocopy, recording, or any other — except for brief quotaions embodied in critical article or printed reviews, without prior permission of the publisher.

Published and Distributed by:

William Carey Library
P.O. Box 40129
Pasadena, CA 91114 USA
Phone: 626.798.0819   Email: publishing@wclbooks.com

Book Layout and Cover Design: D. M. Battermann, R&D Design Services

Third edition, 2001
Printed in the United States of America

Contents

Foreword vii
Preface ix
Peacemaking Passages xi

Part 1:
The Reactive & Restorative Dimensions of Peacemaking

Chapter 1
Biblical Foundations — 3

Chapter 2
The Inverted Pyramid of Peacemaking (Part 1) — 8

Chapter 3
The Inverted Pyramid of Peacemaking (Part 2) — 17

Chapter 4
Preparing for Step One (Private Reproof) — 26 **| Step One:** Private Reproof

Chapter 5
Practicing Step One (Private Reproof) — 29

Chapter 6
Step One (Private Reproof): Confession, Forgiveness & Restoration — 34

Chapter 7
Step One (Private Reproof): Love & Peacemaking — 40

Chapter 8
Step Two: Private Conference — 43 **| Step Two:** Private Conference

Steps Three & Four:
Public Announcement &
Public Exclusion

Chapter 9
   Steps Three and Four: Public Announcement & Public Exclusion   45

Chapter 10
   Overcoming Offense   53
   Developing God Centered Convictions & Grace Oriented Relations

Chapter 11
   Dealing with Leaders   59

Chapter 12
   When Sparks Fly: Conflict and Confrontation Among Leaders   65

Chapter 13
   The Covenant of Forgiveness   69

Part 2:
The Proactive & Preventative Dimensions of Peacemaking

Chapter 14
   Brokenness   79

Chapter 15
   Encouragement & Edification   84

Chapter 16
   Godly Communication   88

Chapter 17
   Wise Communication   93

Chapter 18
   Receptivity to Counsel   96

Chapter 19
   God's Heart for Unity   99

Chapter 20
   God's Hatred of Division   103

Chapter 21
   Spiritual Warfare & Peacemaking   106

Addendum:
   Peacemaking Cross-Culturally   110

Conclusion   112

Part 3:
Peacemaking Applied: **By Elliot Paulson**   117

Bibliography   163

Foreword

In these days of information glut, it is difficult to believe in "the power of the printed page" any more. Even worse, who is into a topical "Bible Study"? Answer: Anyone hungry enough for God and His ways to find the stuff that "slam dunks" us right where we live everyday.

Rick Love's handbook on peacemaking is a slam dunk!

I reflectively read every word in this manual. I filled in the lines. **As a result, I'm equipped to upgrade relationships better than I've ever been.** And I've been "into" reconciliation and intimate relationships for more than 25 years!

Peacemaking isn't a workbook on becoming a nice guy (although that wouldn't be bad for some of us). It's about having *great* friendships that last—which is just what God had in mind all along. As Love writes, "The peace we're pursuing is not just the absence of strife, but rather the development of harmony and intimacy in relationships" with people we don't naturally "click" with.

Let's face it. Even for most Christians, life consists of a whole bunch of mediocre "how-can-I-avoid-her" relationships. This study guide will show you why we don't call sin "sin," and why we don't follow our Creator's specific and totally relevant instructions.

But the most important reason to take in this great study is because, "Blessed are the peacemakers, for they shall be called the sons of God."

Dr. Greg Livingstone
Founder, Frontiers

Preface

I have had the privilege of studying under some of the best theologians and missiologists in America. I learned many valuable lessons about hermeneutics, biblical theology, strategy, culture and contextualization. Yet no one prepared me for peacemaking. This was something I had to learn the hard way—on the job. It has been the most difficult lesson I have learned about church life and church planting.

After serving for ten years as a pastor in America, eight years as a missionary among a Southeast Asian Muslim people group, and six years as an Executive Director of a mission, I am convinced that the Church needs a whole new emphasis on peacemaking. The bulk of my time in the church and in church planting was taken up by peacemaking. I was a peacemaker in marriages (including my own!), among teammates, and in an emerging Muslim convert church. Everywhere I turned, people held grudges, harbored hurt feelings, and experienced broken relationships.

Peacemaking is one of the neglected keys to church life and church planting.

This study has emerged in the context of learning how to become a peacemaker during the past 25 years. I frequently find myself in the midst of peacemaking, but I have to admit I don't like it. Peacemaking is hard work; it's draining. But I do it because *peacemaking is love in action*. The Bible defines love as obedience to Christ's commands (John 15:9-10; 1 John 2:5, 5:3; 2 John 6). In other words, the most loving thing I can do for others is to obey what Christ has taught about peacemaking.

People often ask me how to apply these peacemaking principles in another culture. My answer: true biblical peacemaking does not fit any culture. While every culture values certain aspects of peacemaking, generally peacemaking is "counter-cultural." This is a heavenly message that rubs against the rough edges of earthly cultures.

Certainly how we carry out peacemaking will vary from culture to culture. We must learn the culturally agreed upon ways to communicate and handle conflict. But these ways will almost always fall short of biblical standards.

I have written this as a study guide that can be used for small group Bible studies or individual interaction with the Bible's teaching on this subject. As you wrestle with the text, I pray this guide will help you develop your own convictions about these urgent issues. The best peacemakers are those who have biblical convictions about Christ's approach to right relationships. Because of this, they are willing to do whatever the Bible teaches about promoting peace in the church—for the glory of God!

Dr. Rick Love
International Director
Frontiers

Peacemaking Passages

Matt. 5:9

Matt. 5:23-24

Matt. 6:14-15

Matt. 7:3-5

Matt. 18:15-20

Matt. 18:21-35

Luke 17:3-4

Acts 15:1-35

Acts 15:36-41

Rom. 12:18

Rom. 14:19

Rom. 16:17-18

1 Cor. 5

1 Cor. 6:1-8

1 Cor. 13

2 Cor. 2:10-11

Gal. 2:11-14

Gal. 6:1

Eph. 4:1-3

Eph. 4:15

Eph. 4:31-32

Phil. 4:2-3

1 Thess. 3:6-13

1 Tim. 1:19-20

1 Tim. 5:1-2

1 Tim. 5:19-22

Titus 3:10-11

Heb. 12:14-15

James 3:13-18

James 5:19-20

1 Peter 4:8

Rev. 3:19

The Reactive and Restorative Dimensions of Peacemaking

Part 1

Chapter 1

Biblical Foundations

Peacemaking — resolving conflict, restoring, and building harmony in relationships—is central to church planting. As church planters, we must teach our disciples the "how-tos" of right relationships as summarized in peacemaking.

The priority and importance of peacemaking depends on one's definition of the church. If the church is perceived to be an institution or an organization, then peacemaking isn't central to its life or ministry. Thousands of traditional churches in the United States carry on without carrying out much peacemaking. On the other hand, if you define the church as a community (the body of Christ), then peacemaking is a crucial, urgent need. It is central to church planting. We could summarize its importance in the following syllogism: The church is a community. There is no community without peacemaking. Therefore, peacemaking is central to church planting and church life.

Some people prefer to use the word "reconciliation" to describe the peacemaking process, while others favor the term "church discipline." We will use the terms "peacemaking," "reconciliation," and "church discipline" interchangeably.[1]

Historically, one of the marks of the true church was peacemaking or "discipline"—as summarized in the Belgic Confession of 1561, article XXIX:

> The marks by which the true church is known are these: if the pure doctrine of the gospel is preached therein; if she maintains the pure administration of the sacraments as

Peacemaking:
- ❖ resolving conflict
- ❖ restoring
- ❖ building harmony in relationships.

instituted by Christ; if church discipline is exercised in punishing sin; in short, if all submit herself to the yoke of Christ" (Schaff 3, 419-421:1983).

Two things are worthy of note in this confession—one positive, the other negative. Positively, it highlights the centrality of church discipline in church life. Church discipline is one of the marks of the true church. You cannot have a church without peacemaking. Negatively, it defines the goal of church discipline as punishing sin. Unlike in the New Testament, the Belgic Confession makes no mention of restoring relationships or winning the straying person.

> Church discipline is one of the marks of the true church.

Ronald Wallace makes some pertinent historical observations regarding this negative orientation in church discipline:

> Discipline in the first and second centuries seems to have had the forgiveness and winning back of the erring, rather than their punishment, as its aim … . From the fourth century, discipline began to show undesirable features. More concern came to be shown for the sanctity of the congregation as a whole than for the expelled individual. … the pursuit of discipline became in some quarters more important than the pastoral care of the individual (Wallace 1974:302).

Because of this, modern advocates of church discipline go to great pains to define the more positive dimensions of this peacemaking process. J. Carl Laney says, "Church discipline is God's loving plan for restoring sinning saints" (Laney 1985:14). John White and Ken Blue write about a church discipline that heals (White and Blue 1985). And according to Jay Adams, the purpose of church discipline is "to win the brother, to bring about peace—peaceful relations, peaceful communication, peaceful friendship between two. Brothers ought to be at peace with one another" (Adams 1981:72).

The explicit purpose of peacemaking or discipline according to the

---

1. The terms "reconciliation" and "church discipline" are historically and theologically rich. But they carry communicational baggage. The word "reconciliation" tends to focus attention on the death of Christ and the Godward dimension of peacemaking. Because of this, the more manward or social dimensions of reconciliation could be overlooked. (This should not be the case, however, as Eph. 2:11-22 makes clear.)

The concept of church discipline includes the formal excommunication of believers who have hardened their hearts and refused to be reconciled. Thus, the concept of church discipline is usually linked to formal church leadership and organization. In addition, the term "church discipline" conjures up all sorts of negative feelings and stern connotations. "It's the way that you get rid of troublemakers in church!" Consequently, the positive, relational, non-formal aspects of church discipline may be minimized.

Therefore, the author prefers to use the term "peacemaking."

New Testament is threefold: the glory of God, the welfare of the church, and the restoration of the sinner.

We engage in peacemaking, first of all, to glorify God. He is glorified when unbelievers see our good deeds, and He is blasphemed when they see sin in the church (Matt. 5:16; 1 Peter 2:12; Rom. 2:24). Thus, we promote His glory and honor His name when we keep His commandments and deal with sin biblically.[2] Secondly, the goal of peacemaking is the welfare of the church. We are commanded to guard the purity and unity of the body (1 Cor. 5:1-13; Rom. 15:5-7; 16:17-18; Eph. 4:3; Titus 3:10-11). And finally, the purpose of peacemaking is restoration, to win back an erring brother or sister (Matt. 18:15-17).

The purposes of peacemaking:
- ❖ the glory of God
- ❖ the welfare of the church
- ❖ the restoration of the sinner

While much of the New Testament focuses on the more typical aspects of peacemaking (rebuking, forgiving, restoring), there are cases of excommunication. At Corinth, a man was excommunicated for moral reasons; he was living in an incestuous relationship (1 Cor. 5). First Timothy 1:18-20 describes excommunication for doctrinal reasons. Hymenaeus and Alexander were expelled from the church for their false teaching.

Because we live in a fallen world, the majority of our studies must focus on the **Reactive or Restorative Dimensions of Peacemaking.** "How can we be reconciled once we are alienated?" is the key question in most cases. This is also the emphasis in most books and articles on the subject. It is also the subject of **Part 1** of this study.

However, it is not enough to merely reconcile. We must rebuild and strengthen our relationships. Thus, **Part 2** of this study focuses on the **Proactive or Preventative Dimensions of Peacemaking.** We must learn how to cultivate deeper relationships through encouragement, affirmation and godly communication.

Let's begin with a biblical foundation for peacemaking.

The Biblical Basis for Peacemaking

How is spirituality defined in the New Testament?

> *"Brethren, even if a man is caught in any trespass you who are spiritual, restore such a one in a spirit of gentleness, but watch yourself, or you also may be tempted" (Gal. 6:1).*

Although the New Testament describes spirituality in many ways

---

2. "This is a very serious matter. Since the Lord is jealous for his own honor, if the church does no exercise proper discipline, he will do it himself, as he did at Corinth, where the Lord's discipline resulted in sickness and death (1 Cor. 11:27-34), and as he warned he would do at Pergamum (Rev. 2:14-15) and at Thyatira (Rev. 2:20)" (Grudem 1994:896).

> "Brethren, even if a man is caught in any trespass you who are spiritual, restore such a one in a spirit of gentleness, but watch yourself, or you also may be tempted" (Gal. 6:1).

(abiding in the vine, fighting the good fight, taking up the cross, the fruit of the Spirit, holiness, etc.), Galatians 6:1 clearly underscores the fact that truly spiritual people are peacemakers. They seek to restore those who have fallen into sin or reconcile those who have become enemies. In other words, "the way you and I respond to someone who sins indicates whether or not we are spiritual" (Laney 1985:83).

There are three important aspects of spirituality in this verse: the who, the what and the how. First of all, the who: the context links spirituality with the fruit of the Spirit (Gal. 5:22, 23). Secondly, the what: the characteristics of spirituality listed in the fruit of the Spirit must find expression in the often difficult work of peacemaking. Or conversely, the one who manifests the fruit of the Spirit in his/her life will be a peacemaker! Thirdly, the how: the ministry of reconciliation or peacemaking must be carried out in a spirit of gentleness, humility and vigilance. We must gently restore the erring brother—all the while being on guard, because we ourselves can be tempted.

However, peacemaking is not just for the superspiritual! The whole church is commanded to be involved in the peacemaking process.

❖ Read Rom. 12:18 and summarize what it teaches about peacemaking.

_____

❖ Read Rom. 14:19 and summarize what it teaches about peacemaking.

_____

❖ Read Heb. 12:14 and summarize what it teaches about peacemaking.

_____

❖ Read 1 Peter 3:11 and summarize what it teaches about peacemaking.

_____

> ❖ The word translated "pursue" in three of the verses above is the Greek word, *dioko*, which means "to strive for, aspire to or follow zealously." What does this mean practically regarding peacemaking?
>
> _____
>
> _____

We must be diligent and wholehearted in our pursuit of peace. Peacemaking demands active, persistent effort. And the peace we are pursuing is not just the absence of strife, but rather the development of harmony and intimacy in our relationships.

Thus far, we have seen that peacemaking defines spirituality and is commanded in the New Testament. However, that's not all. God promises a blessing to those who are peacemakers:[3]

> *Blessed are the peacemakers, for they shall be called the sons of God (Matt. 5:9).*

The emphasis of the pronouncement of blessing here is on divine approval more than on our personal happiness (Gundry 1982:68, Carson 1984:131). In other words, peacemakers have the approval of God on their lives! They are called sons (or daughters) of God because they are acting like their Father: the God of Peace (Phil. 4:9, 1 Thes. 5:23) who sent the Prince of Peace (Isa. 9:6) to bring about a world of peace (Luke 2:14). "There is no more Godlike work to be done in this world than peacemaking" (Broadus quoted in Carson 1984:135).

> ❖ How has this study broadened or changed your definition of peacemaking?
>
> _____
>
> _____

---

3. "In light of the gospel, Jesus himself is the supreme peacemaker, making peace between God and man, and man and man. Our peacemaking will include the promulgation of that gospel. It must also extend to seeking all kinds of reconciliation. Instead of delighting in division, bitterness, strife … disciples of Jesus delight to make peace wherever possible" (Carson 1984:135).

Chapter 2

The Inverted Pyramid of Peacemaking (Part 1)

Seeing the Big Picture

The next two chapters introduce the Inverted Pyramid of Peacemaking. This inverted pyramid portrays the primary strands of peacemaking. It helps us see the big picture.

The shape of the pyramid illustrates a primary principle of peacemaking: conflict between people should be kept private. An increasing number of people are included in the process only to help make peace. If there is no repentance or reconciliation, the once private affair becomes progressively public. In other words, peacemaking progresses up the pyramid from private, informal interaction to a formal public process.

This chapter provides a brief look at each part of the pyramid to get a panoramic view of the issues. The rest of the manual will consider each building block in greater detail.

The major building blocks of peacemaking are found in Matthew 18:15-17. Jesus outlines clear-cut steps or guidelines to reconciliation.[4]

> *If your brother sins against you, go and show him his fault, just between the two of you. If he listens to you, you have won your brother over. But if he will not listen, take one or two others along, so that "every matter may be established by the testimony of two or three witnesses." If he refuses to listen to them, tell it to the church; and if he refuses to listen even to the church, treat him as you would a pagan or a tax collector.*

Before we begin to examine the guidelines outlined in the passage, we need to make some general comments on the passage as a whole. First of all, the context of this passage is especially helpful in understanding the purpose of what is normally referred to as "church discipline." As Derek Tidball notes,

> The arrangement of the chapter as a whole is no accident and the location of these particular verses is something like meat in a sandwich. The verses are prefaced by the parable of the lost sheep (18:10-13), which stresses the responsibility of the community actively to seek a weak brother who has strayed. They are followed by the parable of the unmerciful servant (vv. 21-35), which lays upon Christians the obligation to forgive to a totally unreasonable extent. Only if both sides of the sandwich are observed can the discipline of verses 15-20 be truly exercised (Tidball 1986:62).

Thus, these two parables, along with our passage, point out the priority of reconciliation in the body. While it describes church discipline, the primary focus of the passage is on relationships and the restoration of fellowship.

Second, there is no mention of official church leaders in this passage. Reconciliation is not just for leaders. It is something the whole body should be doing.

Third, the quote from the Old Testament in v. 16 ("two or three witnesses") highlights the importance of objectivity and justice in peacemaking. By having more than one witness, misunderstanding, emotional exaggeration, and half truths can be stopped.

Fourth, the issue in this process is not just sin. The issue is that people are not willing to "listen." (The word "listen" is mentioned four times in this passage.) They are not receptive to the counsel of the brethren and are not willing to repent. (This problem will be addressed further in *Chapter 15*.)

Finally, these steps should not be carried out legalistically. We need to go beyond the external behavior of the offender to undercover underlying

---

4. While Jesus outlines clear-cut steps to reconciliation, we do not always have to go through all these steps. If a matter does not originate between two people, we may begin the process of peacemaking at a different stage. For example, in 1 Cor. 5, Paul describes a man at Corinth who was having sexual relations with his stepmother. Because it was a matter of notoriety, Paul pleads with the church to excommunicate the offender. He does not go through the previous steps of peacemaking. "Discipline may begin at any stage in the process. Basically, the rule of thumb by which to determine where the matter should be handled is this: deal with the problem on the level at which it presents itself, making every effort to involve no one other than those already involved" (Adams 1986:37).

motives and attitudes. Thus, we might want to try step one or two a couple of times. Jesus is not giving us a checklist to hurry us through the process. The key phrase in this passage is "if he listens."

Step one in the peacemaking process may involve numerous meetings.

> Perhaps you will find it necessary to try several times before stepping up the process. You may wish to vary your approach. You will want to be sure that you have gone in a spirit of meekness and that you have not alienated him by the manner in which you approached him. You will want to look for signs that he is weakening … . As long as a reasonable discussion of these questions continues, you cannot charge him with failure to listen (Adams 1986:57-58).

An attitude of humility and patience is essential in this whole process.

Jesus outlines four steps in the peacemaking process: private reproof, private conference, public confrontation and public expulsion.

Step One: Private Reproof

> Read Matt. 18:15 and answer the following questions.
>
> ❖ What does the word "brother" imply?
>
> _____
>
> ❖ When are we commanded to go and reprove someone?
>
> _____
>
> ❖ What does it mean to reprove?
>
> _____
>
> ❖ We are to reprove "just between the two of you." Why is this important?
>
> _____
> _____

Some people may feel that they should get someone else's counsel before they reprove their brother. Others may want prayer support. But the Bible pushes us towards private reproof. "You are to tell him his fault 'between you and him alone.' The beauty of Christ's instructions is that they avoid gossip" (White and Blue 1985:90).

> ❖ What is the significance of the phrase, "won your brother"?
>
> _____
> _____

Step Two: Private Conference

The first step of peacemaking is to privately reprove the person who sins. If s/he fails to listen to you, then you need to go to the second step of peacemaking.[5]

> In Matt. 18:16, the operative phrase is "if he won't listen to you." At each stage, what moves the process ahead a step is the refusal of the offender to be reconciled … one moves onto the next step in church discipline only when progress is not being made toward reconciliation because the other person has dug in his heels and is unwilling to do whatever is necessary to be reconciled (Adams 1986:57).

❖ Read Matt. 18:16. How does Jesus describe this private conference?

Notice that the text doesn't say who the witnesses should be. Thus, they do not have to be church leaders. However, it would be wise to have mature people involved (Gal. 6:1). The nature of the sin should probably determine who is involved.

❖ In the second part of v. 16, Jesus quotes from the Old Testament. Why are two or three witnesses needed in peacemaking, according to Jesus?

---

5. "The implication of this Biblical requirement to seek additional help in order to reclaim an offender is that Christians must never promise absolute confidentiality to any person. Frequently, it is the practice of Bible-believing Christians to give assurances of absolute confidentiality, never realizing that they are following a policy that originated in the Middle Ages and that is unbiblical and contrary to scripture (there is not a scrap of evidence in the Bible for the practice) …. Both individuals and counselors must be aware of the all-important fact that *absolute confidentiality prohibits the proper exercise of church discipline* …. We ought to say, 'I am glad to keep confidence in the way that the Bible instructs me. That means, of course, I shall never involve others unless God requires me to do so.' In other words, we must not promise absolute confidentiality, but rather confidentiality that is consistent with Biblical requirements" (Adams 1986:30-32, italics added).

The presence of witnesses gives the reproof added solemnity. They show the offender how serious the issue is. Witnesses also add much needed wisdom and objectivity. They should protect the accused and/or confirm the accusation. "The Biblical requirement of additional witnesses safeguards the judicial process against false accusation, slander, and wrongful incrimination" (Laney 1985:53).

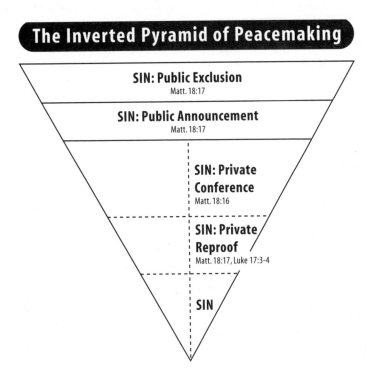

Step Three: Public Announcement

If the person accused of sinning fails to respond to a private reproof (Step One) and then a private conference (Step Two), it may be wise to seek another private conference with him/her. Again, we should not see the four steps of peacemaking as a checklist to hurry through. Our goal is always restoration. However, if progress is not being made toward reconciliation after several attempts, we may need to move to the next steps.

Matthew 18:15-17 clearly describes four steps in the peacemaking process. Some interpreters, however, think that the third and fourth steps describe the one final act of peacemaking: excommunication. In keeping with the four steps described in the text, along with the purpose of peacemaking (restoration), we prefer a four stage approach.

> Read Matt. 18:17 and answer the following questions.
>
> ❖ What is the third step to peacemaking as set forth in the first "if" clause?
>
> _____
>
> ❖ What does it mean, practically, to "tell it to the church"?
>
> _____
>
> _____
>
> _____

The church is the final court of appeal in the peacemaking process. The whole body must be informed. It would be easy to apply this in the early church, since they met in homes. In fact, everyone would probably be aware of the conflict already.

However, it is harder to think about how to apply this in most churches today, which are many times larger than the house churches of New Testament times. The following authors present possible scenarios.

Adams believes that it is "not to be done in the middle of a worship service (in which there is a mixture of believers and unbelievers …) … the world has no right to know about the matter … the church alone must hear … . These considerations mean that one must tell the church either at a closed meeting of its membership … or one does so by telling the elders in their capacity as representatives of the church" (Adams 1986:68-69).

Laney looks at it from a different angle. "I would suggest that no matter how the case is brought before the church, it should be done in such a way that encourages the congregation to find its role in bringing the brother or sister to repentance. The people must be encouraged to pray for the sinner, to avoid a critical spirit and to be aware of the prideful thought, 'That would never happen to me.' The thrust of such a public announcement should be that God hates sin, but loves sinners" (Laney 1985:55).

White and Blue suggest that it might be wise to limit the announcement for two reasons. First of all, up to this point in the passage, there has been a strong personal element to the whole process. Secondly, "First-century churches were largely small house churches. Numbers were probably small by modern standards. People almost always knew one another well. Thus, the church Jesus referred to was the small unit where everything would probably be known anyway. In such a setting, a disciplinary matter that is resisted is *de facto* a community matter. Therefore, it would seem best to interpret Christ's words "to the church" to refer to the particular subgroup with which the offender associates most, if such a group exists. This would avoid exposing the offender to unnecessary humiliation" (White and Blue 1985:128).

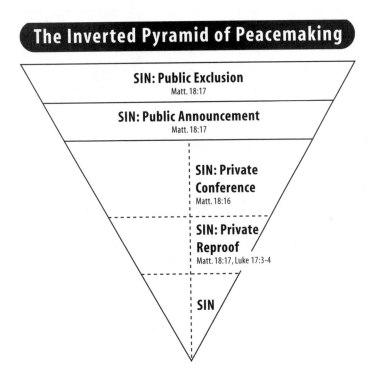

Step Four: Public Exclusion

❖ What is the fourth step to peacemaking as described in the second "if" clause of v. 17?

Pious Jews hated Gentiles and tax-gatherers; they had no social contact. Thus, Jesus was teaching that unrepentant church members must be ostracized from the body. "In ecclesiastical jargon this is referred to as 'excommunication.' The word is derived from the Latin *ex* ('out') and *cummunico* ('share, communicate'). It refers to the cutting off of a person from the church membership, fellowship, or communion. No longer may that person share in the activities and privileges of church membership" (Laney 1985:56).

We must distance ourselves from those excommunicated, much like the Jews related to Gentiles and tax-gatherers. However, like Jesus, we must reject the Jewish "attitude" toward sinners (Luke 7:34; 15:1-3). "We must be careful then that the words "tax collector" and "Gentile" do not cause us to adopt those judgmental and superior attitudes Christ so clearly warns us about. Rather, we are to mourn over tragedy in the body of Christ. We must still leave the door to forgiveness wide open, seeking to win, as Jesus did, those who have been cut off from fellowship by their sin" (White and Blue 1985:97).

We must reiterate two important truths at this point. First of all, the people who are being excommunicated are being excommunicated because of hardness of heart. They refused to listen. (Remember that the word "listen" is mentioned four times in Matt. 18:15-17.) Those who are unreceptive to counsel must be disciplined.

Secondly, it would be helpful to point out again that the explicit purpose of peacemaking or discipline according to the New Testament is threefold: the glory of God, the welfare of the church, and the restoration of the sinner.

> **The purposes of peacemaking:**
> ❖ the glory of God
> ❖ the welfare of the church
> ❖ the restoration of the sinner

Peacemaking is done first of all to glorify God. He is glorified when unbelievers see our good deeds and He is blasphemed when they see sin in the church (Matt. 5:16; 1 Peter 2:12; Rom. 2:24). Thus, we promote His glory and honor His name when we keep His commandments and deal with sin biblically. Secondly, the goal of peacemaking is the welfare of the church. We are commanded to guard the purity and unity of the body (1 Cor. 5:1-13; Rom. 15:5-7; 16:17-18; Eph. 4:3; Titus 3:10-11). And finally, the purpose of peacemaking is restoration, the winning back of an erring brother (Matt. 18:15-17).

Chapter 3

The Inverted Pyramid of Peacemaking (Part 2)

Did you happen to notice some missing blocks in our pyramid? Those empty spaces remind us that there is more to peacemaking than just Matthew 18! While Matthew 18 may be the first word on peacemaking, it is certainly not the last word on the subject. We must understand that passage in light of everything the Bible teaches on the topic.

Sin: The Reason for Reproof

The tip of the pyramid describes the event that makes peacemaking necessary: sin. When people go astray or when relationships sour, reproof becomes necessary. For the glory of God, the sake of the church and the restoration of the sinner, we must act. Peacemaking is a commitment to obey Christ's commands regarding relationships. Peacemaking is love in action.

But is everything that sours relationships or causes division sin?

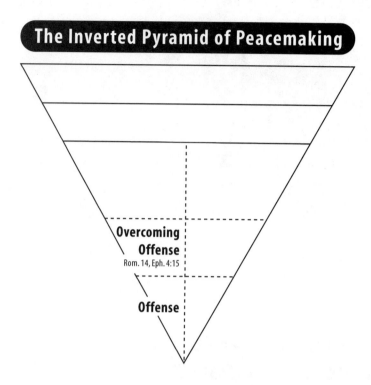

Offense: The "Other" Category

As I reflected more on the issues that cause division, I realized that there is an area rarely mentioned in books on the topic—what I call "offense." I use offense to describe a number of ways relationships can break down: hurt feelings, misunderstanding, different convictions, different personalities, immaturity, and differences in philosophy of ministry. Offense frequently causes rifts in relationships and breaks the bond of unity. It is, therefore, a major peacemaking issue.

Offense can easily lead to sin. In fact, it usually does. That's why there is a dotted line in the Pyramid of Peacemaking between sin and offense.

But offense is not necessarily sin. For example, did Jesus ever cause offense? hurt anyone's feelings? cause misunderstanding? Surely, some Scribes and Pharisees didn't appreciate being called "hypocrites," "blind guides," "whitewashed tombs full of dead men's bones and all uncleanness" (Matt. 23)!

Jesus offended people, hurt their feelings and caused misunderstanding. But he never sinned (2 Cor. 5:21; Heb. 4:15; 1 John 3:5).

Romans 14 addresses similar issues. Paul says, "One person has faith that he may eat all things, but he who is weak eats vegetables only … . One person regards one day above another, another regards every day alike. Each person must be fully convinced in his own mind" (Rom. 14:2,5).

Chapter Three — The Inverted Pyramid of Peacemaking: Part 2

As did the Christians in Rome, so do believers today clash over a variety of personal and theological issues. Differences may offend. Differences are inevitable, but they don't have to cause division.

Thus, Paul warns us that offense may lead to sin: "The one who eats is not to regard with contempt the one who does not eat, and the one who does not eat is not to judge the one who eats, for God has accepted him" (Rom. 14:3).

So how can we overcome the hurt, misunderstanding and differences that so often cause division? How do we deal with offense? Two verses are especially helpful.

Read Eph. 4:3 and answer the following questions.

❖ How does Paul describe peacemaking in this verse?

_____

_____

_____

❖ Why do you think Paul used the word "diligent" (NASB) or the phrase "make every effort" (NIV) to describe the task of peacemaking?

_____

_____

Read Eph. 4:15 and answer the following questions.

❖ Paul begins with the exhortation to "speak." Why is communication crucial to overcoming offense?

_____

_____

_____

> ❖ Why is the communication of truth important in overcoming offense?
>
> _____
>
> _____
>
> ❖ What happens if we speak the truth without love or seek to love someone without truth?
>
> _____
>
> _____
>
> _____

We overcome offense when we communicate in biblical ways. Paul reminds us that the peacemaker must be diligent, making every effort to reconcile relationships. We must resolve to be prompt. We must commit ourselves to persevere.

But overcoming offense is not just a matter of being prompt and persevering. We must also be prepared. We need to prepare our hearts so that we can speak the truth in love.

The Missing Piece: Third-Party Intervention

If an unaccepted private reproof leads directly to private conference with witnesses, what happens in cases of hard-to-overcome offense? Do we grit our teeth and walk away lest offense turn into sin?

Notice the final missing piece in the pyramid: Arbitration, mediation or recourse. This refers to third-party intervention—another respected person steps in to help make peace. A go-between helps reconcile ruptured relations. This third party negotiates between the disputing pair, interpreting the issues for them, and seeking their reconciliation.

According to Augsburger, the experience of mediation "is one of stepping between colliding forces, competing wills and clashing temperaments. Mediation is not only the ability to define and clarify, to separate and discern, to link and reconcile opposites; it is also the capacity to absorb tension, to suffer misunderstanding, to accept rejection, and to bear the pain of others' estrangement" (1992:191).[6]

Moving a dispute to the mediation phase does not necessarily mean that the disputing parties are in sin. It does mean that attempts at private reproof or speaking the truth in love have been unfruitful. Failing communication and growing alienation characterize this level of conflict.

I remember a particularly painful conflict I had with another leader. We had different styles of leadership, some differences in our philosophy of ministry, and little understanding of mediation. When I suggested to

---

6. Mediation is a thoroughly biblical concept. Exactly how the mediator accomplishes the task is culturally conditioned, however. See Augsburger 1992: 156-163, 187-228 and Elmer 1993:65-79 for thought-provoking discussions of mediators and mediation in cross-cultural settings.

this brother that we needed to have our supervisor help us sort out the issues between us he replied, "We have differences, but there is no sin. I forgive you and you forgive me, so according to Matthew 18 we should not have another person involved in our dispute unless we are in sin."

What could I say?

Because we both felt Matthew 18 was the first and last word on peacemaking we resolved to forgive each other and do the best we could to restore our relationship. However, restoration took years! We both wanted to be godly and believe the best of each other, but it took a long time. The pain of conflict went deep. Restoration took time.

In retrospect, I believe we suffered unnecessarily. We needed a mediator badly. We needed a third party to give us perspective. We needed to realize that there is more to peacemaking than Matthew 18!

First Corinthians 6:1-7 and Philippians 4:2-3 describe this important, but often ignored, dimension of peacemaking.

❖ What is the problem Paul faces in 1 Cor. 6:1?

_____

❖ What is Paul's emotional reaction to this problem and why does he feel that way (vs. 1-7)?

_____

_____

_____

❖ Read v. 2b and v. 5 and summarize Paul's concern.

_____

_____

This case at Corinth illustrates the concept of arbitration. Legal disputes among Christians were being brought before unbelieving law courts. Paul insists that these cases should be dealt with in the church.

Arbitration is a legal concept. It refers to the process of having a third party make a binding decision between two disputing parties. The arbitrator determines what each party must do in light of the conflict, giving the final word in the matter.

Chapter Three — The Inverted Pyramid of Peacemaking: Part 2

> ❖ What is the problem Paul faces in Phil 4:2-3?
>
> _____
>
> _____
>
> _____
>
> ❖ How does Paul handle this conflict?
>
> _____
>
> _____
>
> _____
>
> _____

These passages illustrates a case of mediation between two women leaders. (Note that Paul says they "shared my struggle in the cause of the gospel.") Paul confronts Euodia and Syntyche publicly (through this letter) and then asks for a mediator to help them work through their problems.

Recourse

If arbitration is legal, and mediation is relational, then recourse is organizational. Recourse is not explicitly taught in Scripture, but the concept fits with the principles of peacemaking. Recourse means that we can appeal to someone higher up in the organization if we strongly disagree with our supervisor. It does not mean that we go around our supervisor to make our appeal. Rather, recourse means that we go *through* our supervisor to appeal to his/her supervisor. In other words, if several attempts at seeking to speak the truth in love to our supervisor have failed, we then tell our supervisor that we are going to appeal to the person over him/her. We also tell them exactly what we are going to say. In our mission, if we need to resort to recourse, our scattered fields often necessitate that we begin the process via email. If this is the case, we would write our appeal to the higher authority but then copy our supervisor as well.

Godly recourse does not mean we gossip or go around our leadership. We go through them to make our appeal.

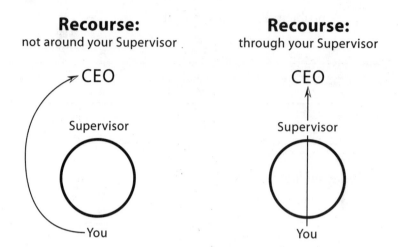

Mediation is a crucial dimension of peacemaking. We need Godly, objective wisdom when we face tangled relationships and unresponsive people. Furthermore, we all need outsiders at times to help us in our relationships. We should actively seek the help of "agreed-upon third parties" to help us be restored to our brothers and sisters. In this way, we can be "diligent to preserve the unity of the Spirit in the bond of peace" (Eph. 4:3). "Blessed are the peacemakers, for they shall be called sons of God" (Matt. 5:9).

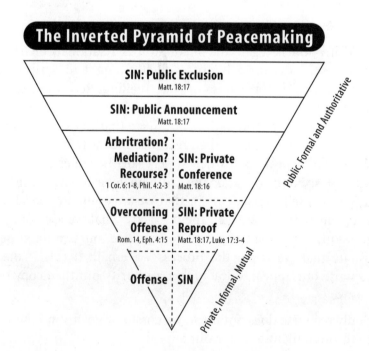

Private, Informal and Mutual Discipline

Peacemaking is a spiritual discipline of Christian community. It is a commitment to obey Christ's commands regarding relationships. As we noted earlier, there is no explicit mention of leaders carrying out discipline in Matthew 18:15-17. It is a mandate for the whole church. Every person in the church needs to obey the "one another" verses. Every person in the church needs to make every effort to preserve the unity of the spirit in the bond of peace (Eph. 4:3). If private, informal and mutual discipline takes place in the church, there will be little need for public, formal and authoritative discipline (defined below).

Private, informal and mutual discipline implies different levels of communication. There is a continuum of approaches of speaking to one another, depending on the relationship and the nature of the sin:

- ❖ Accept one another (Rom. 15:7)
- ❖ Encourage one another (Heb. 3:12-13, 10:24-25)
- ❖ Speak the truth in love (Eph. 4:15)
- ❖ Restore in a spirit of gentleness (Gal. 6:1)
- ❖ Admonish one another (Rom. 15:14)
- ❖ Reprove or rebuke (Luke 17:3)

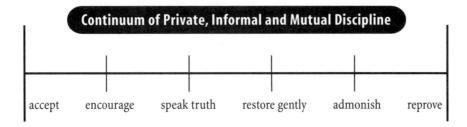

Public, Formal, and Authoritative Discipline

Authoritative discipline refers to the need for leadership intervention when mutual discipline breaks down. This is higher up the pyramid of peacemaking. At this stage of peacemaking, the leadership of the church must act decisively. It is no longer just an issue of restoring the sinner. This is a public, formal and authoritative act. The leaders must guard the purity of the church and the honor of Christ's name by following through on the steps of peacemaking until there is resolution—either repentance or excommunication.

Chapter 4

Preparing for Step One (Private Reproof)

Peacemaking usually breaks down in the first step of the process, described here as private reproof. Because of this we will focus on this first step to peacemaking (private reproof) in the next four chapters.

Our hearts must be prepared for this demanding task.[7]

Glorify God

When we want to apply peacemaking principles practically, we need to begin by seeking to glorify God first of all. Our first priority is to please Him, not just defend ourselves or defeat our opponent. At Corinth, Paul faced a divided church. There were moral, legal and dietary disputes in the congregation. What was his response?

Whether, then, you eat or drink or whatever you do, do all to the glory of God (1 Cor. 10:31).

"Biblical peacemaking is motivated and directed by a desire to please and honor God. His interests, reputation, and commands should take precedence over all other considerations" (Sande 1992:8). What is paramount in peacemaking is our commitment to loving God by obeying His commands.

*If your brother sins against you, go and show him his fault, just between the two of you. If he listens to you, you have won your brother over. But if he will not listen, take one or two others along, so that "every matter may be established by the testimony of two or three witnesses." If he refuses to listen to them, tell it to the church; and if he refuses to listen even to the church, treat him as you would a pagan or a tax collector.
Matt. 18:15-17 (NIV)*

---

7. We will follow Ken Sande's four practical guidelines to peacemaking outlined in *The Peacemaker*. *The Peacemaker* is a handbook for conflict resolution. It is an excellent, comprehensive, practical guide to peacemaking. As a lawyer, however, he tends to put a great emphasis on the more legal dimensions of the process rather than the pastoral.

A God-centered approach to peacemaking is not just focused on results, for sometimes people don't respond to reproof. Thus, if people don't respond positively to our efforts at reconciliation, we can find comfort and encouragement knowing that we are pleasing God. As noted earlier, God's "interests, reputation, and commands should take precedence over all other considerations" (Sande 1992:8).

> ❖ Why do you think glorifying God is a crucial first step?
>
> _____
>
> _____
>
> ❖ What might happen in peacemaking if we did not seek to glorify God first of all?
>
> _____
>
> _____

Get the log out of your own eye

> Read Matt. 7:1-5 and answer the following questions.
>
> ❖ Summarize the main point of vs. 1-4 in your own words:
>
> _____
>
> _____
>
> ❖ Note the words "first" and "then" in v. 5. What does this teach us about confronting others about their sin?
>
> _____
>
> _____
>
> _____

Jesus forbids premature or improper confrontation. We must first face up to our own sins and faults. Then we are able to confront our brother.

> In the brotherhood of Jesus' disciples, censorious critics are unhelpful. But when a brother in a meek and self-judg-

ing spirit (*cf.* 1 Cor. 11:31; Gal. 6:1) removes the log in his own eye, he still has the responsibility of helping his brother remove his speck (*cf.* Matt. 18:15-20) (Carson 1984:184).

There is one additional point we should make regarding this step. In many situations, the road to reconciliation is simple: overlook minor offenses.

> ❖ Read Prov. 19:11. What does this teach us about "getting the log out of our own eye"?
>
> _____
>
> _____

Make every effort to overlook inconsequential wrongdoing.

Since God does not deal harshly with us every time we sin, we should be willing to treat others in a similar fashion. While this does not mean that we must overlook all sins, it does require that we make every effort to overlook inconsequential wrongdoing. This should take place under two conditions. First, the offense should not have created a wall between you and the other person ... . Second, the offense should not be doing serious harm to God's reputation, to others, or to the offender (Sande 1992:63-64).

> ❖ In what way do these two guidelines (glorify God, get the log out of your own eye) cause you to search your own heart and challenge your motives?
>
> _____
>
> _____
>
> ❖ Why do you think purity of heart is important in peacemaking?
>
> _____
>
> _____
>
> _____
>
> _____

Chapter 5

Practicing Step One (Private Reproof)

A God-centered approach to peacemaking means that we are committed to doing things His way, for His glory, regardless of the outcome. To be God-centered also means that we are sin-sensitive. We want to reprove ourselves (remove the logs in our eyes), before we reprove anyone else. Then we are ready to do private reproof.

Matt. 5:23-24 gives us important teaching about the first step of reconciliation. Read this passage and answer the following question.

❖ Who is responsible to take initiative in the peacemaking process? (Note the words, "if your brother has something against you.")

_____

_____

We are commanded to take the initiative—even if our brother/sister is the one who "has the problem." We are not allowed to wait for this person to come to us. If we are aware that someone appears to be cold toward us or struggling in their relationship with us, then we must go to them!

> ❖ Notice the words, "first" and "then" in v. 24. What does this tell us about the priority God puts on peacemaking?
>
> _____
>
> _____

The context of these verses is worship. We are commanded to stop in the middle of a worship time, and worship (Rom. 12:1-2) by obedience—in other words, to reconcile with a brother or sister if there is something wrong between us. Reconciliation is more important than church services.

> These words clearly indicate that there is an urgency to reconciliation. God says, "go first." Indeed, in Christ's example, reconciliation takes precedence over worship. Surely that must be one of the striking features in the example chosen; by using so bold a contrast as that between worship and reconciliation, He intended to underscore the importance and the priority of reconciliation. Unreconciled relationships, therefore, constitute *emergency priorities* that may not be handled casually or at one's leisure" (Adams 1973:53).

We cannot truly worship God if we are not in right relationship with our brother/sister. This strong link between loving God and loving our brother/sister is also emphasized in 1 John. "The one who says he is in the light and yet hates his brother is in the darkness until now" (1 John 2:9). "If someone says, 'I love God,' and hates his brother, he is a liar" (1 John 4:20).

> Read Luke 17:3-4 and answer the following questions.
>
> ❖ These verses include three conditions or possibilities (note the "if"). Write them out:
>
> _____
>
> _____
>
> _____

> - These verses also include three commands related to the three conditions or possibilities mentioned above. Write out the three commands:
>
>   _____
>
>   _____
>
> - What does this passage teach us about nursing grudges or criticism?
>
>   _____
>
>   _____

This passage forbids the nursing of grudges and criticism. We are commanded to both rebuke and forgive. And this forgiveness must be without limit.

> When Jesus speaks of *seven times in the day* He does not, of course, mean that an eighth offense need not be forgiven … forgiveness must be habitual. From the world's point of view, a sevenfold repetition of an offense in one day must cast doubt on the genuineness of the sinner's repentance. But that is not the believer's concern. His business is forgiveness (Morris 1974:256).

> Read Gal. 6:1 and answer the following questions.
>
> - What are spiritual people supposed to do in this verse?
>
>   _____
>
> - What does the word "restore" imply about the process of peacemaking?
>
>   _____
>
>   _____

The discipline of a saint is not designed to punish or destroy, but rather to "mend" and "repair" someone who has been injured or damaged on the battlefield of life (Laney 1985:86).

> ❖ How are we supposed to restore people?
> _____

Gentleness "is a condition of the heart and mind which evokes courteous, considerate, thoughtful and humble dealings with others. It is the opposite of pride, self-assertiveness and self-interest" (Laney 1985:87).

> ❖ Summarize the main points of peacemaking as noted in all of the verses above:
> _____
> _____
> _____
> _____
> _____
> _____
> _____
> _____

Step One in Practice

- **Start the confrontation on a positive note.** Affirm before confronting. Tell the person whom you are confronting what you appreciate about him/her. Mention concrete things s/he has done to be a blessing to you or others. This was Jesus' approach to the churches in Revelation 2-3. People need to sense your love and concern for them personally.

  > Start with the positive.
  > Begin with questions.

- In some cases, a person's sin is obvious. However, it is usually wise to **begin the process of reconciliation with questions.** Go in a spirit of gentleness (Gal. 6:1) and do not attack the other person. Put the onus on yourself. For example: "Maybe I'm misunderstanding … but I'm sensing something is wrong between us. Have I done said or done something that I need to get right with you?" If the person has not sinned against you personally, you might ask, "John, maybe I'm misperceiving the situation, but I'm sensing that something is wrong here because … . Am I observing this situation correctly?"

- What have you learned from this study that you need to put into practice?

  _____

  _____

  _____

  _____

Chapter 6

Step One (Private Reproof): Confession, Forgiveness and Restoration

Confessing Your Sin

The ultimate goal of peacemaking is peace—overcoming differences, resolving conflicts, restoring, and building of harmony in relationships. For this to happen, sin must be dealt with biblically. Reproof is only part of God's formula. Confession and forgiveness are also integral.

First of all, there needs to be **confession** of sin to God and to anyone who has been sinned against. "As a general rule, you should confess your sins to every person who has been directly affected by your wrongdoing" (Sande 1992:95). If you have sinned against one person in private, then you should confess your sins to him in private. If you have sinned publicly, you should confess your sin to everyone involved. If you have sinned mentally (*e.g.*, lust or envy) you should confess to God alone, since it does not directly affect others.

In some cases, confession of sin must lead to restitution for the wrongs done: "When a man or woman commits any of the sins of mankind ... he shall confess his sins which he has committed, and he shall make restitution in full for his wrong and add to it one-fifth of it, and give it to him whom he has wronged" (Num. 5:6-7; see also Lev. 6:2-7; Luke 19:8). The principle of restitution comes into play when there are material damages, not over personal offense or hurt.[8] Confession of sin alone is sufficient when the offense is personal.[9]

Forgiveness

It is not enough to say "I apologize" or "I'm sorry" when we confess our sins. Confession of sin must always be linked with forgiveness. The sinner must confess his sin, ("I have sinned by _____. Will you forgive me?") and the person sinned against must forgive.[10] Thus, *forgiveness* is the second dimension to the reconciliation process.[11] When one asks, "Will you forgive me?" he has punted; the ball has changed hands, and a response is now required of the one addressed. The onus of responsibility has shifted from the one who did the wrong to the one who was wronged. Both parties, therefore, are required to put the matter in the past. And the proper response (Luke 17:3) is, "Yes, I will." Like God's forgiveness ("Your sins and iniquities I will remember against you no more"), human forgiveness is a *promise* that is *made* and *kept* .... When one person says, "I forgive you" to another, he promises: 1. "I'll not bring this matter up to you again;" 2. "I'll not bring it up to others;" 3. "I'll not bring it up to myself (*i.e.*, dwell on it in my mind)" (Adams 1979:222).

Forgiveness is not a feeling. Neither is forgiveness forgetting someone's sins. "When God says that he 'remembers your sins no more' (Isa. 43:25), He is not saying that He cannot remember our sins. Rather, He is promising that He will not remember them" (Sande 1992:162). Thus, forgiveness is a choice, an act of the will, whereby we promise that we will not bring up the matter again.[12]

---

8. See Sande, pp. 217-219, for a summary of the Biblical teaching on restitution.

9. Certain kinds of sins, such as adultery, however, demand more than just confession of sin. The one who has fallen into adultery must be restored by "putting off the old man" (ungodly habits and sin patterns) and "putting on the new man" (holy habits and righteous behavior). This involves, at the very least, the renewal of the mind and various types of accountability. The adulterer must re-establish trust with his/her spouse by proving his/her repentance. That is, a new lifestyle must indicate a true change of heart and habit.

10. This is not a legalistic formula. We are merely offering concrete practical steps on how to reconcile biblically. What is important in these steps is that guilt is acknowledged and forgiveness is communicated. If you can think of better ways to communicate these two essential dimensions of reconciliation, please let the author know.

11. One of the most comprehensive and practical studies on forgiveness is by Jay Adams, *A Theology of Christian Counseling*, Grand Rapids: Zondervan Publishing House, pp. 184-232.

12. See "The Covenant of Forgiveness" on page 69 for a practical tool outlining these steps.

Forgiveness is commanded in Scripture. We must forgive others just as Christ has forgiven us: "And be kind to one another, tenderhearted, forgiving each other just as God in Christ also has forgiven you" (Eph. 4:32). "Forgiving each other, whoever has a complaint against anyone; just as the Lord forgave you, so also should you" (Col. 3:13).

But perhaps forgiveness is best illustrated in the following passage.

Read Matt. 18:21-35 and answer the following questions.

❖ What is the point of vs. 21-22?

"In rabbinic discussion, the consensus was that brother might be forgiven a repeated sin three times; on the fourth, there is no forgiveness. Peter, thinking himself big-hearted, volunteers seven times" (Carson 1984:405). But the whole point of Jesus' answer was to teach a formula of limitless forgiveness.

❖ How does the king deal with the first slave in vs. 23-27?

❖ How does the first slave deal with his fellow slave in vs. 28-30?

❖ How does the king deal with the wicked slave in vs. 31-35?

> ❖ Summarize the point of vs. 33 and 35:
>
> _____
>
> _____

Verses 21-35 "emphasize the priority and the unlimited application of forgiveness in the area of a disciple's personal relationships. It is a different subject from that of vv. 15ff. [on church discipline], but one which is an essential complement ... . The proper severity of v. 17 [excommunication] must be balanced by a forgiving attitude which reflects the disciple's own experience of much greater forgiveness" (France 1985:276-277).

Restoration: Rebuilding Broken Relationships

Confession and forgiveness mark a turning point in a broken relationship. Reconciliation is established. Fresh beginnings are possible. However, restoration is rarely automatic, especially if the relationship has had chronic or severe problems.

Usually there is a season, after the promise of forgiveness is granted, where both parties still "feel" uncomfortable around each other. While both parties may have sincerely repented and forgiven each other, memories of past pain lurk beneath the surface of our consciousness. Emotional scars remain tender, old patterns of relating endure.

Thus, more than forgiveness is necessary for true restoration. Rebuilding broken relationships is not easy. It takes time. Trust must be re-established; new ways of relating established. Practical avenues of affirmation and encouragement must be attempted.

The simple illustration on the next page might help explain what happened and what needs to happen to make true peace. First, the relationship is broken. Then, forgiveness is granted. Finally, the relationship needs to be restored.

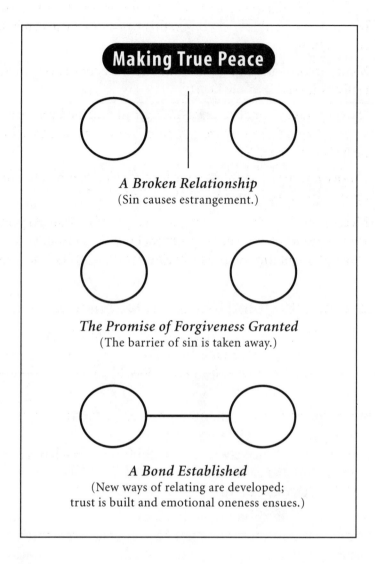

A few practical suggestions can help you go beyond reconciliation to restoration:

1. Remember that both forgiveness and restoration are things of the heart.

2. Claim James 5:16 in prayer: Confess your sins to one another and pray for one another *so that you may be healed*. We need other brother and sisters holding us accountable and praying for us. Healing in relationships takes place when we walk in the light (confessing our sins) and when we pray.

3. Jesus said, "Where your treasure is, there will your heart be also" (Matt 6:21). This teaches us the principle of investment. You must begin to invest prayer, time and energy in developing a new relationship with the person. Spend time talking. Find activities that

Chapter Six— Step One: Private Reproof - Confession, Forgiveness and Restoration

you can do together that will help you interact with each other without awkwardness. If you do this, your heart will catch up with your actions.

4. Meditate on and pray over what Peter teaches about love, especially as it relates to the heart:

"Since you have in obedience to the truth purified your souls for a sincere love of the brethren, fervently love one another from the heart" (1 Peter 1:22).

"Above all, keep fervent in your love for one another, because love covers a multitude of sins" (1 Peter 4:8).

5. Meditate on Phil. 4:8 as it relates to the formerly estranged person. Let your mind dwell on what is positive about the person. Learn to take "every thought captive to the obedience of Christ" (1 Cor. 10:5).

❖ What aspect of this study was most helpful to you?

_____

_____

_____

❖ Which of these three steps is most difficult for you?

_____

_____

_____

❖ What area do you need to work on?

_____

_____

_____

Chapter 7

Step One (Private Reproof): Love & Peacemaking

Confronting or rebuking someone is never easy. A thousand and one excuses pop into our minds telling us not to confront a person about sin. This is normal, but it is neither biblical nor loving.

In fact, peacemaking is love in action.

In this study, we will continue to look at the first step to peacemaking in light of what the Bible teaches about love. In other words, *what is the relationship between peacemaking and love?*

> ❖ The first thing we need to do to understand what the Bible teaches about love is to read the second commandment in its original context. Read Lev. 19:18. Note the contrast ("but") in the verse. What is love contrasted with in this verse?
>
> _____
>
> ❖ In light of these contrasts, how is love originally defined?
>
> _____
>
> _____

Chapter Seven— Step One: Private Reproof - Love and Peacemaking

In the original giving of the second commandment, love is defined as the opposite of taking revenge or bearing a grudge. Thus, love is defined in concrete terms as overcoming grudges. Read Lev. 19:17 if you want to know one practical way to overcome grudges!

As L. De Koster notes, "Discipline due [in the sense of the first step of peacemaking], but ignored is not love but *sentimentality*, love's counterfeit" (De Koster 1990:238).

> Discipline due, but ignored is not love but *sentimentality*, love's counterfeit.

❖ Read 1 Cor. 13:4-6. Which aspects of love are *directly related* to peacemaking in these verses?

_____

_____

_____

Read 1 Peter 4:8 and answer the following questions.

❖ What is the significance of the phrase "above all"?

_____

❖ What does the phrase "keep fervent" teach us about love?

_____

❖ What does Peter mean by saying "because love covers a multitude of sins?"

_____

_____

Here are some practical ideas for application. First of all, pray for God's love for the person who is offending you. Meditate on verses about love and ask God to help you love the person you are struggling with. This is what it means to be fervent in your love for one another.

In many cases, God gives you victory and your love for that person does cover a multitude of sin. On the other hand, if you have obeyed 1 Peter 4:8 and you still feel as though there is a barrier between you and the offender (or if there is serious sin that needs confrontation), you need to apply Rev. 3:19.

❖ Read Rev. 3:19. What is the proof of Christ's love for the church in this verse?

_____

❖ Since Christ is our model, what is the proof of our love for someone else?[13]

_____

❖ Quickly re-read the verses on love mentioned in the box above. Choose the verse that is most relevant to you (the area you need to work on or the area you need encouragement in). Write the verse below, then stop and prayerfully meditate on that verse.

_____

_____

_____

_____

_____

_____

_____

_____

---

13. See also John 15:9-10 and 2 John 6. In both passages love is defined in terms of obeying God's commandments. Thus, the most loving thing we can do for a brother and sister is to obey the commandments on peacemaking and seek to restore or be restored to our brother or sister.

Chapter 8

Step Two: Private Conference

Jesus exhorts us to privately reprove the brother or sister who sins. If s/he fails to listen to us, then we need to go to the second step of peacemaking: private conference. We invite respected others to join us in the process of confronting sin and facilitating reconciliation:

"But if he does not listen to you, take one or two more with you, so that by the mouth of two or three witnesses every fact may be confirmed" (Matt. 18:16).

❖ Read Deut. 19:15-19 (the original basis for Matt. 18:16). What was the purpose of witnesses according to v. 15?

_____

❖ What is the role of the judge according to v. 18 and what does this imply for participants in the private conference?

_____

_____

❖ Why is thorough investigation necessary, according to this passage?

_____

The role of the third party in peacemaking demands careful listening, thorough investigation, and objective evaluation of the facts. Prov. 18 gives wise guidelines in this quest.

> ❖ What are the implications of Prov. 18:2 for private conference?
>
> _____
>
> _____
>
> ❖ What are the implications of Prov. 18:13 for private conference?
>
> _____
>
> _____
>
> ❖ What are the implications of Prov. 18:17 for private conference?
>
> _____
>
> _____
>
> ❖ How does step two (private conference) apply in a marriage context? If one person continually confronts an unresponsive spouse about sin, what should s/he do according to Matt. 18:16?
>
> _____
>
> _____
>
> ❖ What aspect of this lesson was most helpful to you?
>
> _____
>
> ❖ What will be difficult for you to apply?
>
> _____
>
> _____
>
> Stop now and ask the Lord to help you.

Chapter 9

Steps Three & Four: Public Announcement & Public Exclusion

Paul the apostle did not give a systematic step-by-step procedure for peacemaking as Jesus did. Nevertheless, scattered throughout his letters are references to both the teaching and the practice of peacemaking in his congregations. Much of his general teaching is focused on the first step to peacemaking. ("Speak the truth in love," "Be diligent to preserve the unity of the Spirit," "Pursue the things which make for peace," and so forth—teaching that we will examine more thoroughly in Part 2 of this study guide.)

But he does make a few significant references to excommunication. It may be that Paul's teaching describes the same process as Matthew 18, only in different words. Or he may be speaking of sterner measures because of differing problems. At the very least, his terminology is different. Instead of public announcement and public exclusion, he describes a discipline of avoidance and deliverance over to Satan. [14]

---

14. See Rom. 16:17-18; Titus 3:10-11, 2 Thes. 3:6-13, and 2 John 10-11 for further teaching about excommunication. These verses contain stern warnings about divisiveness, laziness and false teaching.

Disciplining the unrepentant

> Read 1 Cor. 5:1-8 and answer the following questions.
>
> ❖ Describe the situation that Paul is facing.
>
> _____
>
> _____
>
> ❖ Why is Paul concerned about sin in the church according to vs. 6-8?
>
> _____
>
> _____
>
> ❖ What do you think Paul meant by delivering someone over to Satan? (See also 1 Tim. 1:20.)
>
> _____
>
> _____
>
> ❖ By the phrase "the destruction of the flesh?"
>
> _____
>
> _____

These are obviously difficult concepts for the modern church. However, most commentators agree that "delivering over to Satan is an act of discipline for unrepentant sin and involves putting the person out of the church, the fellowship of God's people, into the realm controlled by Satan" (Knight 1992:111).

The phrase "the destruction of the flesh" is problematic. After a thorough, painstaking analysis, Gordon Fee concludes, "What Paul was desiring by having this man put outside the believing community was the destruction of what was 'carnal' in him, so that he might be 'saved' eschatologically" (Fee 19:212).

A careful comparison of 1 Cor. 5:5 and 1 Tim. 1:20 indicates that while excommunication may appear radical, a redemptive or remedial emphasis is clearly in view. Both verses have clear purposes: "that they may be saved;" "that they may be taught not to blaspheme."

That God should use Satan and the world as a whip to spank His rebellious children should be no surprise to those who are conversant with the Old Testament. Time and again, that is the message of the Old Testament books (Adams 1986:79).

Read 1 Cor. 5:1-13 and answer the following questions.

❖ How is excommunication described in vs. 2, 5, 11, 13?

_____

_____

_____

_____

(Note: The reason for excommunication—the purity of the church—is mentioned by Paul in 1 Cor. 5:6-8.)

Reasons for excommunication

Church history records many bad examples of church discipline. People have all too often been excommunicated for secondary issues, even mere differences of opinion. However, while there have been and will be abuses, the teaching and exercise of church discipline is demanded in Scripture.

Jesus commends the church at Ephesus because it did not tolerate evil men (Rev. 2:2) and reproves the churches at Pergamus and Thyatira for tolerating false teaching and evil in their midst (Rev. 2:14, 20). Moreover, the New Testament records various examples of sins subject to church discipline: sexual immorality (1 Cor. 5:1); false teaching (1 Tim. 1:20; 2 John 10-11); divisiveness (Rom. 16:17; Titus 3:10), and laziness (2 Thes. 3:6-15).

The discipline of lazy people appears to be a unique category in this list. It does not warrant expulsion from the church like the other sins, but is nevertheless considered formal discipline. At Thessalonica some believers were living unruly or undisciplined lives. Since they were not working, they were disobeying apostolic practice and teaching (2 Thes. 3:6-10).

We can only speculate about the reasons for laziness. Were these new believers exploiting the love of the Thessalonican church? Were they overly influenced by Greek culture which did not value manual labor? Or were they too preoccupied with the impending return of Christ to think of work? Whatever their reasons, there were no valid excuses for their lifestyle. According to Paul, the church must "keep away from every brother who leads an unruly life and not according to the tradition" (2 Thes. 3:6). They were to take special note of these people and not associate with them (2 Thes. 3:14).

However this did not mean that they were excommunicated from the church, for Paul hastens to add: "Yet do not regard him as an enemy, but admonish him as a brother." To take special note of a lazy member and not associate with him or her could mean a number of things: removal from office, refusing the person leadership opportunities or teaching privileges, not allowing the person to take communion, and so forth. At the church in Thessalonica, it probably meant the offender would not receive food and drink from the church.

What sins actually merit excommunication? What is the biblical basis for disciplining someone out of the church?

As we mentioned earlier, the people who are being excommunicated are being excommunicated because of hardness of heart. They refused to listen. (Remember that the word "listen" is mentioned four times in Matt. 18:15-17.) Those who are unreceptive to counsel must be disciplined.

However, excommunication can be abused. Authoritarian leaders may want to discipline someone out of the church simply because they are not obeying (based on Heb. 13:17). Thus, churches that exercise church discipline must be careful to discipline its members according to specific sin patterns described in Scripture.

Paul gives us clear guidelines in 1 Cor. 5:11-13:
> But actually, I wrote to you not to associate with any so-called brother if he is an immoral person, or covetous, or an idolator, or a reviler, or a drunkard, or a swindler—not even to eat with such a one. For what have I to do with judging outsiders? Do you not judge those who are within the church? But those who are outside God judges. Remove the wicked man from among yourselves (1 Cor. 5:11-13).

In other words, when a person lives like an unbeliever s/he should be treated as such. Discipline is necessary. The following passages provide similar guidelines:
> Or do you not know that the unrighteous will not inherit the kingdom of God? Do not be deceived: neither fornicators, nor idolaters, nor adulterers, nor effeminate, nor homosexuals, nor thieves, nor the covetous, nor drunkards, nor revilers, nor swindlers, will inherit the kingdom of God (1 Cor. 6:9-10).

> Now the deeds of the flesh are evident, which are: immorality, impurity, sensuality, idolatry, sorcery, enmities, strife, jealousy, outbursts of anger, disputes, dissensions, factions, envying, drunkenness, carousing, and things like these, of which I forewarn you, just as I have forewarned you, that those who practice such things will not inherit the kingdom of God (Gal. 5:19-21).

> But immorality or impurity or greed must not even be named among you, as is proper among saints; and there must be no filthiness and silly talk, or coarse jesting, which are not fitting, but rather giving of thanks. For this you know with certainty, that no immoral or impure person or covetous man, who is an idolater, has an inheritance in the kingdom of Christ and God. Let no one deceive you with empty words, for because of these things the wrath of God comes upon the sons of disobedience (Eph. 5:3-7).

Wayne Grudem wisely summarizes:

> A definite principle appears to be at work: all sins that were explicitly disciplined in the New Testament were publicly known or outwardly evident sins, and many of them had continued over a period of time. The fact that the sins were publicly known meant that reproach was being brought on the church, Christ was being dishonored, and there was a real possibility that others would be encouraged to follow wrongful patterns of life that were being publicly tolerated (1994:896-897).

Restoring the repentant

The Bible gives us clear guidelines on how to excommunicate a brother or sister in sin. But what should the church do when an excommunicated brother or sister repents?

Apparently, a brother was excommunicated from the Corinthian church (after Paul's urging—1 Cor. 5) and later repented. Because of this, Paul gave the church at Corinth some clear teaching on how to restore a repentant brother or sister.

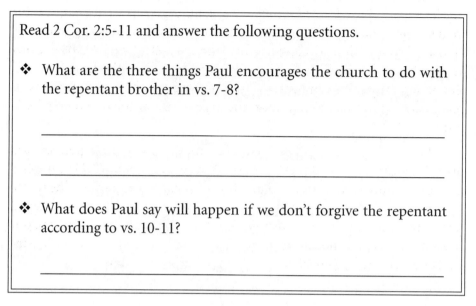

The Corinthian church had rightly excommunicated a brother but had failed to restore him after he repented. Paul exhorts them to forgive him, comfort him and reaffirm their love for him. But Paul not only exhorts them positively. He also warns them. If they do not forgive this brother, Satan can take advantage of them. Lack of forgiveness is an open door for the devil, a breeding ground for demonic bondage.

> Formal reinstatement must be made as publicly as dismissal was, and in the same manner if possible. The Prodigal Son was given a robe, a ring, and a party in his honor, showing us that joy should accompany the return of the son who was lost, but now is found (Adams 1986:96).

The Authority of the Church and Peacemaking

The verses immediately following the classic passage on peacemaking, Matt. 18:18-20, are understood by many as the basis for warfare praying and intimate fellowship. Most Christians take this as a blanket promise of power through prayer and communion with the living Christ. However, the context clearly connects these promises with peacemaking.

For those who know the tensions and burden of peacemaking, these verses are enormously comforting. Here we have promises of spiritual authority, answered prayer and Christ's own presence in the peacemaking process!

First of all, we have the promise of spiritual authority. In peacemaking, the authority of heaven intersects with the church's decisions regarding excommunication. Church discipline has heavenly support and sanction. A look at the Greek terms and tenses used makes this clear.

Jesus links excommunication with the concepts of binding and loosing. The words "bind" and "loose" were technical terms used by the rabbis in decision making. "Binding" meant to prohibit or declare unlawful, "loosing" to permit or declare lawful (Gundry 1982:336, 368-369). Consequently, in this passage, "to bind" means to withhold fellowship. It is the power of excommunication. "To loose" means to forgive. It refers to readmission into the church upon the repentance of the one being disciplined.

The Greek tenses in this verse are noteworthy. Future perfects are used: "shall have been bound" or "shall have been loosed." This implies that our future acts of discipline (future tense) already have heavenly sanction (perfect tense) because we are agreeing with already established heavenly standards. In other words, "It is the church on earth carrying out heaven's decisions, not heaven ratifying the church's decisions" (Rienecker and Rogers 1980:49).

Second, in v. 19, Jesus points out the secret of wise decision making in church discipline: agreement and prayer. As Laney notes,

> Those who prayerfully seek God's wisdom in exercising discipline may have confidence that the decisions they make reflect the will of God in heaven ... . The verb "agree" suggests the idea of coming to agreement by talking over a matter. This means that plenty of interaction and discussion is necessary in formulating the prayer request ... . Instead of making decisions on the basis of a majority vote ... Jesus is setting forth the principle of decision-making based on consensus and unanimity. This is especially important in matters relating to church discipline, for disagreement on such matters will result in dissension, internal strife, and criticism of leaders (Laney 1985:75-76).

Finally, Jesus links peacemaking with His presence. Jesus is present in the disciplining process so that the decisions made on earth have heavenly sanction. In summary, "Christ is saying, 'I give you authority to exercise church discipline, permitting and prohibiting those things that I have either authorized or forbidden in My Word. You exercise My authority and heaven itself backs you up'" (Adams 1986:114).[15]

---

15. Paul likewise emphasizes the divine presence and authority of Christ in peacemaking. Regarding church discipline in Corinth, he affirms that it is done "in the name of the Lord Jesus...with the power of our Lord Jesus" (1 Cor. 5:4).

❖ Summarize in your own words the most important aspects of peacemaking you learned from this study. What new insights, if any, did you gain?

_____
_____
_____
_____
_____
_____
_____
_____
_____

❖ What will be the most difficult for you to carry out?

_____
_____
_____
_____
_____
_____

Chapter 10

Overcoming Offense: Developing God-Centered Convictions & Grace-Oriented Relations

How do we handle valid differences in the body of Christ? How can we keep non-sin issues from dividing us? In what areas can we agree to disagree? There are no simple answers. But the Scriptures do address these important subjects.

As noted earlier, one area rarely mentioned in books on peacemaking is what I call "offense." Offense refers to hurt feelings, misunderstanding, different convictions, different personalities, immaturity, and differences in philosophy of ministry. Offense frequently causes rifts in relationships and breaks the bond of friendship. It is, therefore, a major peacemaking issue.

Offense can easily lead to sin. In fact, it usually does. That's why there is a dotted line in the Inverted Pyramid of Peacemaking between sin and offense. But offense is not necessarily sin.

Christians in Rome clashed over different convictions. Divisions arose between the strong (those with liberty of conscience) and the weak (Jewish Christians with a scrupulous commitment to dietary regulations and holy days). Questions about diet and days hardly seem important to us today. But in the early church, these issues threatened to fracture the fellowship.

Paul's teaching on the subject gives us helpful guidelines to overcome valid differences of opinion. He encourages both God-centered convictions and grace-oriented relations. In doing so, he reminds us that while many of our cherished beliefs may be valid, they should never disrupt the unity of the fellowship.

One of the important themes of this passage is Paul's insistence that beliefs about diet and days are non-essentials that should not divide us. We must be careful that we don't elevate non-essentials, especially issues of custom and ceremony, to the level of essential and make them tests of orthodoxy and conditions of fellowship (cf. Stott 1994:358).

Let's explore what these two groups believed and what Paul encourages them to do to address these issues.

> ❖ Read Rom. 14:1-15:7 and answer the following questions. What did the weak believe (Rom. 14: 2, 5)?
>
> _____
>
> _____
>
> ❖ What did the strong believe (vs. 2, 5)?
>
> _____
>
> _____
>
> ❖ What does this passage teach us about our different convictions or beliefs (vs. 4, 5, 10, 12, 14, 22)?
>
> _____
>
> _____
>
> _____
>
> ❖ Do you think Paul sided with the weak or the strong in terms of theological convictions (Rom. 14:14, 16, 17, 20)?
>
> _____
>
> _____
>
> _____

❖ How does Paul exhort each party (the strong and the weak) to treat each other (Rom. 14:1, 3, 4, 10, 13, 15, 19, 20, 15:2, 7)? List his main points.

_____

_____

_____

_____

_____

_____

_____

Paul reminds the Romans that both the strong and the weak must hold their convictions before God. They must cultivate **God-centered convictions**: "Each person must be fully convinced in his own mind" (Rom. 14:5), "For we will all stand before the judgment seat of God … each one of us will give an account of himself to God" (Rom. 14:10, 12). Yet he also admonishes them to develop **grace-oriented relations**: "accept the one who is weak in faith … let us not judge one another anymore … pursue the things which make for peace and the building up of one another … do not tear down the work of God for the sake of food … each of us is to please his neighbor for his good, to his edification … accept one another" (Rom. 14:1, 13, 19, 15:2, 7).

In summary, "faith instructs our own conscience; love respects the conscience of others. Faith gives liberty; love limits its exercise" (Stott 1994:375).

According to the Reformers, Romans 14 taught about non-essentials, *adiaphora*, "matters of indifference," whether (as here) involving diet and days, or secondary beliefs which are not part of the gospel. Distinguishing between the essentials and non-essentials in Christian doctrine and practice is no easy task, as the history of denominationalism and church splits give testimony. What is an essential doctrine for one church is a non-essential to another and vice versa. How do we deal with the vast diversity of doctrine and practice among evangelicals? How can we practically hold to God-centered convictions and grace-oriented relations?

Clearly defining what we mean by essential and non-essential is a good starting point. Let's start with a controversial example to get the theological juices flowing! I believe that all the gifts of the spirit are operative in the church today. This is an extremely important doctrine to me personally. In fact, I would argue with great passion and painstaking exegesis that this is exactly what the Bible teaches.

But I would not consider this an essential doctrine to the Christian faith. Many godly, gracious believers in the church differ with my interpretation. I count them as dearly beloved brothers and sisters in Christ. For example, I have earned two degrees from Westminister Theological Seminary in Philadelphia—a seminary that explicitly denies the present operation of certain spiritual gifts.

Admittedly, I have faced the temptation to judge them or not accept them warmly. And I know that many in their camp face the same temptation with me. In addition, I am not a member of a church that holds their view on charismatic gifts, nor would I want to serve on the same church planting team with people holding this view.

But I recognize that we agree on the major doctrines of the Christian faith: The full humanity and divinity of Christ, salvation by grace through faith alone, the Trinity, the divine authority and inspiration of Scripture, and so forth. These essentials refer to the basics of the Christian faith—those doctrines that the church has agreed upon throughout its history, such as the Apostles' Creed, the Nicene Creed, and the Chalcedonian Creed. Therefore, we are family. I can enjoy their fellowship.

According to John Stott, we discern the essentials from the non-essentials as follows: "A safe guide is that truths on which Scripture speaks with a clear voice are essentials, whereas whenever equally biblical Christians, equally anxious to understand and obey Scripture, reach different conclusions, these must be regarded as non-essentials" (1994:374).

Let's look at one more illustration using Stott's guidelines. We could say that belief in the second coming of Christ is an essential doctrine, while the doctrines of the pre-tribulation rapture or pre-millennialism are non-essential. The church with one voice has declared its faith in the second coming of Christ throughout history. However, specific doctrines of the end times such as the pre-tribulation rapture or pre-millennialism have no such consensus. This does not mean that the pre-tribulation rapture or pre-millennialism are unimportant. Nor does it mean that these doctrines lack vigorous defenders! In fact, these are defining doctrines for a large segment of the Evangelical church. However, adherence to these doctrines cannot be considered as tests of orthodoxy nor conditions of fellowship. Not all points of doctrine are equally important (Matt. 23:23). [16]

❖ What are some of the non-essential beliefs that threaten the unity of the church today?

_____
_____
_____
_____
_____

❖ What non-essentials have kept you from deeper fellowship with someone?

_____
_____
_____
_____
_____

❖ According to Rom. 14:1-15:7 what do you need to do about it?

_____
_____
_____
_____
_____

16. Even such a staunch conservative Calvinist as J. Gresham Machen agrees to doctrinal diversity. According to Machen, areas of valid doctrinal differences include views on the millennium, sacraments, church government and even Arminianism (1994:48-51)! See John Frame's *Evangelical Reunion* for a thought-provoking, balanced and wise analysis of these same issues (1991:84-98).

This well-known poem captures the intent of Romans 14:
> In essentials unity;
>
> In non-essentials liberty;
>
> In all things charity.

Chapter 11

Dealing with Leaders

Noah got drunk. Abraham lied. Moses murdered a man. David committed adultery and murder. Peter and Barnabas compromised gospel truths when Jewish legalists came to town. Euodia and Syntyche couldn't get along, and Diotrephes usurped authority. The Bible is clear. Leaders are not perfect. They, too, need to be confronted about their sin.

In this study, we will examine the issue of peacemaking among leaders. It is crucial that we know how to confront sinning leaders in a biblical manner, whether they be pastors, elders, bosses, spouses or parents. We will examine four ways to deal with leaders according to 1 Tim. 5 and Titus 1. We must appeal to them, honor them, rebuke them publicly, and (at times) reprove them severely.

> The Bible is clear. Leaders are not perfect. They, too, need to be confronted about their sin.

Appeal to them.

Read 1 Tim. 5:1-2 and answer the following questions. This passage focuses only indirectly on confronting leaders, in that leaders may be older than we are.

> ❖ What is the contrast in v. 1 and what does it teach us about confronting people?
>
> _____
>
> _____
>
> ❖ How are we to confront older men and women?
>
> _____
>
> _____
>
> ❖ How are we to confront younger men and women?
>
> _____
>
> _____
>
> ❖ Why do you think Paul uses family imagery when discussing confrontation in this passage?
>
> _____
>
> _____

Paul urged Timothy to avoid a harsh, insensitive treatment which would not appreciate their age. The term "rebuke," mentioned only here in the New Testament, describes a severe verbal pounding ... . The term "exhort" [appeal] demands a kinder, more considerate approach than the previously mentioned "rebuking" (Lea and Griffin 1992:145).

While we must be kind and gentle when confronting those older than we are, it is important to note that we must confront them. Confronting an older person or one who is in authority over us is considered anathema in most cultures. It was in Paul's day. But the option is not *whether* we should confront sin in an older person. We must. The option is *how* we confront those older than us.

George Knight's comparison of extrabiblical documents in light of this passage is illuminating.

> Extrabiblical documents ... give advice on how to relate to various groups ... . Two important differences mark Paul's

words here in comparison with such documents. First is Paul's command that Timothy "appeal to" or "exhort" the various groups, especially older members. The other documents are concerned only with the honor to be given and the proper relationship of younger to older, and do not even consider the question of instruction by one who is younger. *The keynote of this passage is the responsibility and authority of a minister of God to give such instruction, albeit to give it with respect, and this makes it different from those accounts in its most central aspect.* Secondly, the other documents speak of three categories: those older, peers, and those younger, whereas this passage speaks of only two categories: those older and those younger. The other documents say that younger men are to be treated as sons; in our passage they are to be treated as brothers. Here, the Christian teaching of the brotherhood of believers is evident. The differences are more significant than the similarities (Knight 1992:215 emphasis added).

Therefore, peacemaking knows no boundaries of age. We are to humbly and gently confront those who are older than we are, and we are to graciously confront those who are younger.

Honor them.

Read 1 Tim. 5:17-18 and answer the following questions. These verses do not directly deal with confronting a leader, but the verses immediately following these verses do. Thus, before Paul explains how to impartially reprove elders who are sinning, he describes how the church is to genuinely care for its elders.

> ❖ Is Paul modeling the importance of affirmation before confrontation—much as Jesus does in Rev. 2 and 3?
>
> _____
>
> ❖ How is the task of an elder described in v. 17?
>
> _____
>
> ❖ An elder is to receive double honor. What do you think this means, especially in light of v. 18?
>
> _____
>
> _____

Rebuke them publicly.

Read 1 Tim. 5:19-21 and answer the following questions.

> ❖ What guideline does Paul give in v. 19 regarding confronting an elder? Why is this an important guideline?
>
> _____
>
> _____
>
> ❖ How are we to confront a sinning leader according to v. 20?
>
> _____
>
> ❖ Why do we rebuke them publicly according to v. 20?
>
> _____
>
> ❖ What is the main point of v. 21 and why is v. 21 crucial to Paul's exhortation?
>
> _____
>
> _____

In summary, Paul emphasizes three principles in the handling of accusations against leaders. First, he stresses *fairness*. We must be guided by the objective criteria of two or three witnesses. Second, disciplining leaders involves *boldness*. If the accused has sinned, s/he must receive a public rebuke. Thirdly, there must be *impartiality*. Timothy is reminded that he carries out discipline in the very presence of God.[17] No vendettas or favoritism allowed!

If this seems harsh, we must remember that those who rule well are to be doubly honored. If they sin as leaders, they bring public dishonor to the name of Christ and hence, must be publicly rebuked.

---

17. The God-centered aspect of peacemaking is worth noting. This is the third passage in which the presence of God is linked with peacemaking (Matt. 18:20, 1 Cor. 5:4, 1 Tim. 5:21).

Reprove them severely.

> Read Titus 1:13 and answer the following questions.
>
> ❖ How are we to reprove false teachers? (See also Titus 2:15.)
>
> _____
>
> _____
>
> _____
>
> ❖ What is the goal of reproof?
>
> _____
>
> _____
>
> _____
>
> _____

According to the context, Titus must reprove these false teachers severely ("correct them rigorously," Fee 1988:180), because their error was grave. Consequently, in certain settings, the normal course of gentle rebuke must give way to a more stern approach. Yet even this severity has positive ends: it should aim at the goal of restoration: "that they may be sound in their faith."

> ❖ Summarize in your own words the most important aspects of peacemaking you learned from this study. What new insights, if any, did you gain?
>
> _____
>
> _____
>
> _____
>
> _____
>
> _____

❖ Have you ever needed to confront a leader about sin? What would you do differently as a result of this study?

_____

_____

_____

_____

_____

Chapter 12

When Sparks Fly: Conflict and Confrontation Among Leaders

Paul and Barnabas: Differences in Philosophy of Ministry

The apostles called him the son of encouragement (Acts 4:36). "He was a good man, and full of the Holy Spirit and faith" (Acts 11:24). We know him as Barnabas.

Barnabas mentored the zealous new convert named Paul. Barnabas stood by Paul when older believers feared him; he recruited Paul when young believers needed him (Acts 9:26-27; 11:22-26). Later, Barnabas humbly submitted to Paul's leadership on their first missionary journey (Acts 13-14).

But something happened as they prepared for their second missionary journey together.

❖ Read Acts 15:36-41 and answer the following questions. What words does Luke use to underscore the intensity of the difference?

_____

_____

_____

❖ What was the reason for the sharp disagreement between Paul and Barnabas?

_____

_____

_____

❖ Could there be some differences in philosophy of ministry that caused this clash? In other words, what motivated Barnabas and what motivated Paul?

_____

_____

❖ What was the result of their conflict, and what can we learn from it?

_____

_____

_____

_____

_____

_____

Leaders disagree, sparks fly and teams divide. Is this always a bad thing? Is it ever OK to "agree to disagree"? Horace Fenton makes three important observations regarding the conflict between Paul and Barnabas. (1) Accept the fact that differences can happen. (2) Find a temporary solution. (3) Look for healing in the long run (1987:107, 110, 113). This is good advice.

But I would add a fourth point: (4) Find a mediator who can help make the separation as gracious as possible.

Chapter Twelve —When Sparks Fly: Conflict and Confrontation Among Leaders

Paul and Barnabas needed a respected mediator to help them work out their differences. This mediator, or go-between, would probably not have persuaded them to change their perspectives. But he could have helped them minimize the pain of separation. A mediator could keep them from exacerbating an already difficult situation.

It is encouraging to note that Paul, Barnabas (and Mark) were eventually reconciled. After this separation, Paul refers to Barnabas in positive terms as a co-worker for Christ (1 Cor. 9:6). Near the end of his life, Paul exhorts Timothy: "Pick up Mark and bring him with you, for he is useful to me for service" (2 Tim. 4:11).

At times, godly men and women, with differences in philosophy of ministry, need to agree to disagree. Rather than striving to maintain one team, it is sometimes wise to divide up into two. The sagacious mediator must encourage them to hold to their God-centered convictions, while being grace-oriented in their relations (Rom. 14).

Paul and Peter: When Truth is Worth Fighting For

> ❖ Read Gal. 2:1-14 and answer the following questions. Why did Paul go up to Jerusalem (v. 2)?
>
> _____
>
> _____
>
> ❖ How did the leadership of the church of Jerusalem respond to Paul's gospel and ministry (vs. 6-10)?
>
> _____
>
> _____
>
> _____
>
> ❖ What were Paul's motivations for this bold confrontation of Peter (vs. 11-14)? List them all carefully.
>
> _____
>
> _____
>
> _____
>
> _____

> ❖ What are some practical things we can learn from this confrontation?
>
> _____
>
> _____

This obviously intense confrontation between these two great apostles must have been stunning. Here was the classic case of an irresistible force meeting an immovable object. But this was no mere difference of personality, culture or philosophy of ministry. *Paul confronted Peter over the truth of the gospel* (Gal. 2:14; cf. Gal. 2:5)! He called Peter on the carpet for denying the truth and acting like a hypocrite. Peter the rock stood on sinking sand.

Thankfully, most conflicts don't fit into this category. Rarely are we called upon to confront another leader about such fundamental truths. But if we are, let's not just imitate Paul's confrontation. Let's also imitate his preparation. He had submitted his personal theological convictions to the leadership of the Christian community and received their commendation (Gal. 2:1-10). Before you confront another leader over an area of truth, check your position with other leaders. Let the confrontation come after the community's commendation!

Chapter 13

The Covenant of Forgiveness [18]

The covenant of forgiveness provides practical biblical guidelines for community of life. This covenant involves a commitment to four fundamental aspects godly relationships especially outlined in Matt. 18:15-35 and Prov. 9:8, 10:17, 11:14, 12:1, 15. We commit ourselves to

- reprove
- be reproved
- repent
- forgive

Those who yield themselves to this pattern of peacemaking will experience reconciliation and find themselves substantially changed through the process.

The Covenant Defined

Forgiveness is a promise. Thus, it falls under the category of a covenant. The covenant of forgiveness is practiced between two parties: the sinner (the one causing the hurt through sin) and the sinned against (the one absorbing the pain). Forgiveness is a gracious act consisting of a threefold promise:

- A promise that the sinned against will not throw up the crime in the face of the sinner in the future in order to gain some advantage.

---

18. This chapter on the covenant of forgiveness was developed jointly with Dick Scoggins.

❖ A promise that the sinned against will not be talking about the crime to others and thus injure the sinner. (In that case, the sinned against would become the sinner and would need to exercise the sinner's part.)

❖ A promise that the sinned against will not rehearse the incident over and over again in his/her mind, thus "nursing the grudge." This perhaps is the most difficult thing to do for someone in this habit. However, a review of 2 Corinthians 10:3-5 and Philippians 4:8 will show that this is possible, although it may take some practice.

The Covenant Exercised

The following example will presume it is exercised in a marriage relationship between a husband (in this case the sinner) and the wife (in this case the sinned against). But the same would apply to children and parents, problems in the church body, and so forth.

1. Reprove: In the event that the sinner does not know that he is the sinner, the sinned against approaches the sinner in love, having first removed the logs from her own eyes and seeking the good of the sinner (Matt. 7:1-5). She then points out how she has been sinned against.

If the sinner is in a position of authority over the sinned against (as in the case of children approaching their parents), the sinned against needs to approach the person with respect. (See 1 Tim. 5:1-5.)

2. Be Reproved: The sinner, having already agreed upon the importance of reproof (Prov. 9:8, 10:17, 11:14, 12:1, 15), has committed himself to be open to correction. When approached by his wife, he listens carefully to her reproof.

3. Repent: The sinner ideally sees his sin and takes full responsibility for it. He acknowledges no place for blame shifting or excusing his actions based on the sin of another. He realizes he is responsible to act righteously and also react righteously (*cf*. Rom. 12:17-21). The correct response for the sinner is repentance toward God and confession toward the sinned against. The correct confession is: "I was wrong for _____. (He names the sin). Will you forgive me?" Note that the sinner does not say, "I am sorry," although he may be. If the sinner refuses the light, or if he excuses or justifies the action, the relationship remains compromised. In the case of an erring Christian, it will be necessary for the sinned against to take the next steps in Matthew 18.

4. Forgive: Upon seeing the sincere humility of the sinner, the sinned against, filled with the Holy Spirit and in full knowledge of the great forgiveness God has granted to her when she deserved only condemnation, says, "I forgive you," thus making the covenant.[19]

The correct confession is: "I was wrong for (name the sin). Will you forgive me?"

Chapter Thirteen — The Covenant of Forgiveness

Note: The covenant of forgiveness was written especially to help those sinned against to walk in the Spirit even if the sinner has not repented. As Paul says, "If possible, so far as it depends on you, be at peace with all men" (Rom. 12:18). The phrase, "so far as it depends on you" indicates that we are responsible to do all that we can do to pursue peace, whereas the phrase "if possible" indicates that it will not always be possible to be at peace with all men.

> While you must forgive in your heart and not carry bitterness against another, you may not *grant* him forgiveness (*i.e.*, promise not to bring up the matter again) until he repents. Otherwise, you could not carry the matter on through the other steps of discipline were it necessary to do so (Adams 1986:53-54).

❖ Does the covenant of forgiveness above describe the way that you typically handle your role as the sinned against? (Think of specific examples.)

_____

_____

_____

_____

❖ How about your role as the repentant sinner? Do you make it a practice to confess, "I was wrong for _____?" Or do you just say, "I'm sorry?" What is the difference between the two?

_____

_____

_____

_____

_____

---

19. The sinned against will often want to cross examine the sinner to test whether his repentance is genuine. It is natural and even good for the sinned against to seek verification of the sinner's humility. If the sinner's sin is habitual or a life dominating problem, it will take further counseling and training in righteousness to bring about the change necessary for a true oneness of relationship. This will often take place in a discipling relationship with a mature brother (in the case of the husband). If the sin persists and the husband ignores it, the wife should proceed to the next step of peacemaking.

Three Types of Conflict Response

People generally respond to conflict in one of three ways. There are conflict provokers, conflict controllers and conflict avoiders. These three personality types are not right or wrong in and of themselves. Each can be Spirit led or fleshly. These three types appear to be related to personality traits and/or the Spirit's gifts.

1. Conflict Provoker (The Prophet)

Strength:
Allows no grudges.
Weakness:
Polarizes people.
Burden:
Walk in the light!

The conflict provoker does not intentionally provoke conflict, but rather prophetically exposes conflict and challenges people to deal with conflict—immediately. The strength of this type is that they do not allow people to nurse grudges or walk in darkness. The weakness of this position is that s/he might expose something but not know how to deal with it properly so that ultimately the problem gets exacerbated and the parties experience much unnecessary pain. The conflict provoker is insensitive to timing in confrontation, sees everything as black or white, and often polarizes people in conflict. The burden of the person with this type of gifting or personality can be summarized in the command: "Walk in the light!"

2. Conflict Controller (The Pastor)

Strength:
Prayerful reflection.
Weakness:
Manipulates situations.
Burden:
Walk in wisdom!

The conflict controller does not intervene in a conflict until s/he can figure the best way to bring about healing and reconciliation. The strength of this type is their pastoral concern to prayerfully reflect on the issues prior to confrontation to insure a wise handling of the situation. The weakness of this position is that s/he manipulates situations for his/her own ends or according to his/her own limited perspective. This can stifle the positive creativity and synergistic results that conflict can bring. The burden of the person with this type of gifting or personality can be summarized in the command: "Walk in wisdom!"

3. Conflict Avoider (The Mercy Show-er)

Strength:
Overlooks transgressions.
Weakness:
Minimizes sin.
Burden:
Walk in grace!

The conflict avoider's highest value is harmony. Thus, this person does everything in his/her power to avoid conflict. The strength of this type is that s/he believes that "love covers a multitude of sins" (1 Peter 4:8). This personality type is a mercy show-er who models Solomon's wisdom: "A man's discretion makes him slow to anger, and it is his glory to overlook a transgression" (Prov. 19:11). The weakness of this type is that it often minimizes sin and seeks peace at any price. While we must always seek to overlook inconsequential wrong doings, superficial healing or false harmony will result when we fail to confront sin (Luke 17:3; Rev. 3:19). The burden of the person with this type of gifting or personalitycan be summarized in the command: "Walk in grace!"

- ❖ Which type of conflict response best describes your pattern?

  _____

- ❖ If you are married, can you identify your spouse's conflict response pattern?

  _____

- ❖ If unmarried, can you identify the pattern of a team leader, close co-worker, boss?

  _____

- ❖ Think of a past conflict situation and your response to it. How did that situation illustrate the strengths and weaknesses of your response to conflict?

  _____

  _____

  _____

  _____

  _____

  _____

STOP GOSSIP!

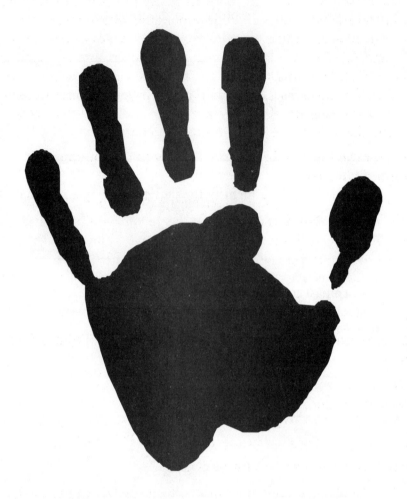

Dealing with gossip and criticism are central aspects of peacemaking. If we teach the following "five finger approach" (each finger representing one principle) to those whom God has given us to lead, our ministries will be greatly enhanced. These principles will also save many others from much undue pain.

If someone comes to you with gossip or says something negative about someone else …

1. Don't believe everything the person tells you.

The Bible commands us to "examine everything carefully; hold fast to that which is good" (1 Thes. 5:21). The wise person gets all the facts: "He who gives an answer before he hears, it is folly and shame to him" (Prov. 18:13). "The first to plead his case seems just, until another comes and examines him" (Prov. 18:17).

2. Say something positive about the person or the situation.

The person who came to you with gossip just planted negative seeds in your mind about someone. By responding with something positive, you are helping to break the vicious cycle of sin that causes so much alienation and division. We are commanded to "overcome evil with good" (Rom. 12:21). And sins of the tongue are very evil (James 3:6). Eph. 4:29 says, "Let no unwholesome word proceed from your mouth, but only such a word as is good for edification according to the need of the moment, that it may give grace to those who hear."

3. Encourage the gossiper to go directly to the person who offended him/her.

You need to remind the gossiper/negative talker of the biblical responsibility to go directly and privately to the person who has sinned against them. "And if your brother sins, go and reprove him in private" (Matt. 18:15). "If your brother sins, rebuke him; and if he repents forgive him" (Luke 17:3; see also Matt. 5:23-24). Ask the gossiper specifically when s/he plans to go to the offending party, and tell him/her that you will hold him/her accountable to do so.

4. Offer to go with the person to facilitate reconciliation, if necessary.

It is always best to have the person go privately to reconcile, according to Matt.18:15. But at times a third party may be needed. This was commended by Paul in 1 Cor. 6:1-5 and approved by Jesus: "Blessed are the peacemakers, for they shall be called sons of God" (Matt. 5:9).

5. Remind them that God hates gossip!

God hates "the perverted mouth" (which surely includes gossip; Prov. 8:13). Three of the seven things the Lord explicitly hates deal with sins of the tongue "The Lord hates ... a lying tongue ... a false witness who utters lies and one who spreads strife among brothers" (Prov. 6:16-19).

❖ Think of a recent situation when you were approached with gossip or negative talk. How did you respond?

_____

_____

_____

_____

❖ What difference would it have made in the situation if you had used the "five finger approach" described here?

_____

_____

_____

_____

_____

_____

_____

❖ Summarize in your own words the most important aspects of peacemaking you learned from this lesson. What insights, if any, did you gain?

_____

_____

_____

_____

_____

_____

_____

_____

_____

_____

The Proactive and Preventative Dimensions of Peacemaking

Part 2

Chapter 14

Brokenness

In the second part of this study guide, we will examine the proactive and preventative dimensions of peacemaking. Remember that we define peacemaking as resolving conflict, restoring, and building harmony in relationships. The focus in Part 2 of this study guide is building harmony. As we encourage and edify one another, we develop harmony, we strengthen relationships, and we minimize the normal strains and stresses in our relationships.

Most of the New Testament focuses on this positive aspect of peacemaking. All of the "one another" verses in the New Testament, for example, emphasize this dimension of peacemaking. As we love one another, serve one another, pray for one another, accept one another, and forgive one another, there will be peace in the body. But we must begin Part 2 with an important topic that is not usually associated with peacemaking—brokenness.

Brokenness and Peacemaking

Brokenness in this study is best captured by the Webster's dictionary definition: "crushed; humbled; as a broken spirit; subdued, tamed; trained as a broken colt."

Thus, we are using the term "brokenness" in a positive sense, not in the negative sense of being wounded.

Peacemaking:
- ❖ resolving conflict
- ❖ restoring
- ❖ building harmony in relationships.

> Brokenness describes the attitude of a person who is humble and quick to repent.

The words "broken" or "brokenness" are not often found in Scripture, although the concept pervades the Bible. Brokenness describes the attitude of a person who is humble and quick to repent. A broken person has died to self. To be broken is to let God be God in every area of your life. As Roy Hession says, "Brokenness is a yielded heart open before God, a heart emptied of pride and self claims, of all arrogance, knowing our sin, our self deception, our frailty, weakness and inadequacy … . Brokenness is not the opposite of wholeness; it is the continuing precondition for it" (Hession 1977:40). And because our self-centered flesh is never fully conquered, we must continually be broken.

Brokenness is a crucial dimension to peacemaking. Although it is primarily a Godward transaction, brokenness before God leads to sensitivity with others. In this way, an atmosphere of brokenness on a team or in a church greatly enhances peacemaking. It is very easy to make peace with humble people! Broken people are receptive to counsel and approachable. Broken people seek to reprove others gently, for they are quite aware of their own sin and need for forgiveness. Brokenness, therefore, is foundational to the proactive and preventative dimensions of peacemaking.

Read Ps. 51:16-17 and answer the following questions.

❖ What is the contrast between vs. 16 and 17?

_____

❖ What is the sacrifice that pleases God?

_____

❖ Define what you think brokenness means according to these verses.

_____

_____

Read Isa. 66:1-4 and answer the following questions.

❖ How is brokenness described in v. 2b?

_____

Chapter Fourteen — Brokenness

- ❖ Notice the first clause in v. 2b ("But to this one I will look," NASB, or "This is the one I esteem," NIV). What does this teach us about how God views His people?

  _____

  _____

- ❖ Compare this verse with 1 Peter 5:5 and Isa. 57:15. What does this mean practically?

  _____

- ❖ What do vs. 1 and 2a teach us about God?

  _____

- ❖ How does this relate to brokenness?

  _____

- ❖ Why do you think Isaiah describes sacrifices in such startling terms in v. 3? And how does this relate to brokenness?

  _____

- ❖ What is the connection between v. 4 and brokenness?

  _____

Brokenness takes place in our relationship with God. According to Hession, "Brokenness in daily experience is simply the response of humility to the conviction of God. And inasmuch as this conviction is continuous, we shall need to be broken continually. And this can be very costly, when we see all the yielding of rights and selfish interests that this will involve, and the confessions and restitutions that may be sometimes necessary" (Hession 1977:23).

Alan Nelson's view is similar: "The breaking process is that which convicts a person of his or her sin, or stubbornness, or insensitivity to God. It renders the soul responsive" (Nelson 1994:27).

Brokenness =
- ❖ *humility* before God
- ❖ *sensitivity* to sin, others
- ❖ *receptivity* to Scripture, counsel

Thus, brokenness is the pathway to spiritual depth, godly character and healthy relationships. According to the verses above, brokenness before God manifests itself in a profound humility before a holy, awesome God.

> ❖ Prayerfully read through the chart on the next page.[20] Ask God to speak to you specifically about relationships you need to work on and areas where you need to be broken.
>
> _____
> _____
> _____
> _____
> _____
> _____
> _____
> _____
> _____
> _____
> _____
> _____

---

20. This is a modification of a similar handout. I could not find the name of the original author.

Brokenness

Proud People	**Broken People**
have a critical, fault-finding spirit; look at everyone else's faults with a microscope, but their own with a telescope.	are compassionate; can forgive much because they know how much they have been forgiven.
have an independent, self sufficient spirit.	have a dependent spirit; recognize their need for others.
have to prove that they are right; have a demanding spirit.	are willing to yield their rights and the right to be right.
are wounded when others are promoted and they are overlooked.	are eager for others to get the credit and rejoice when others are lifted up.
are self-centered; keep others at arm's length.	are other-centered; take the risk of loving intimately.
are unapproachable or defensive when criticized.	receive criticism with a humble, open spirit.
have a hard time saying, "I was wrong, will you please forgive me?"	are quick to admit failure and to seek forgiveness when necessary.
wait for the other to come and ask for forgiveness when there is a misunderstanding or conflict in the relationship.	take the initiative to be reconciled, no matter how wrong the other may have been.
are concerned primarily about the consequences of their sin.	are grieved over the cause, the root of their sin.
are concerned with being respectable, with what others think; work to protect their own image and reputation.	are concerned with being real; what matters to them is not what others think but what God knows; are willing to die to their own reputation.
compare themselves with others and feel worthy of honor.	compare themselves to the holiness of God and feel a desperate need for His mercy.

Chapter 15

Encouragement & Edification

In this study, we will look at the importance and priority of encouragement and edification in peacemaking. The key New Testament word for encouragement is *paraklesis* (the noun) or *parakaleo* (the verb), which has three shades of meaning: to exhort, to encourage or to comfort. (The focus of this lesson is on the last two meanings, since comfort is really a form of encouragement.) The word usually translated "edification" is *oikodome* (the noun) or *oikodomeo* (the verb), which means to build up, to strengthen or to edify.

Two spiritual gifts are directly related to the ministry of encouragement and edification. The spiritual gift of exhortation, described in Romans 12:8, uses the Greek word *paraklesis*. The gift of prophecy contains elements of both *paraklesis* and *oikodome*. For example, in 1 Cor. 14:3, Paul defines prophecy in terms of edification (*oikodome*) and exhortation (*paraklesis*) and consolation. (Compare also 1 Cor. 14:12, 26, 31 and Acts 15:32.)

In addition, there are many examples of encouragement and edification in the early church. Barnabas was nicknamed "the son of encouragement" (Acts 4:36) because he would stand by young, controversial disciples and encourage them on. He did this with both Paul and Mark (Acts 9:26-27; 15:39). He was also forever encouraging the church: "When he [Barnabas] had come and witnessed the grace of God [at the church at Antioch], he rejoiced and began to encourage (*parakaleo*) them all with resolute heart to remain true to the Lord" (Acts 11:21).

Paul often sent fellow workers to encourage the church. He sent Tychicus to the church at Ephesus that he might encourage (*parakaleo*) their hearts (Eph. 6:22). He sent Tychicus on another encouraging mission to the church at Colossae that he might encourage (*parakaleo*) their hearts (Col. 4:8). And he sent Timothy to the church at Thessalonica to encourage (*parakaleo*) them in their faith (1 Thes. 3:2). Paul himself often encouraged (*parakaleo*) his young churches (Acts 14:22; 16:40) and was himself encouraged by the brethren: "But God ... comforted/encouraged (*parakaleo*) us by the coming of Titus" (2 Cor. 7:8).

> ❖ Envision one of these church planting "encouragement" visits. Describe what you think Barnabas, Tychicus, Timothy, or Paul actually did or said to encourage the young church.
>
> _____
>
> _____
>
> _____
>
> _____

It is worth noting that Paul also described his apostolic ministry in terms of "building" (*oikodome*). Twice he mentions the authority the Lord gave him in terms of "building up" (1 Cor. 10:8, 13:10). And in Rom. 15:20, he describes his famous passion for pioneer missions: "And thus, I aspired to preach the gospel not where Christ was already named, that I might not build (*oikodomeo*) on another man's foundation."

Thus, both encouragement and edification were central aspects of pioneer church planting. Moreover, both are necessary in the proactive and preventative dimension to peacemaking.

> Read Heb. 3:12-13 and answer the following questions.
>
> ❖ Who are we exhorted to encourage (*parakaleo*) and how frequently?
>
> _____
>
> ❖ Why is encouragement such a crucial ministry according to these verses?
>
> _____

❖ How does encouragement function proactively and preventatively in the peacemaking process according to these verses?

_____

_____

Read 1 Thes. 5:11 and answer the following questions.

❖ What are we commanded to do in v. 11?

_____

❖ How does encouraging (*parakaleo*) or building others up (*oikodomeo*) enhance our relationships?

_____

_____

Read Rom. 14:19 and answer the following questions.

❖ What are we commanded to pursue?

_____

❖ How does pursuing peace and the things that build up (*oikodomeo*) enhance peacemaking?

_____

_____

Read Eph. 4:29 and answer the following questions.

❖ What are the two commands in this verse?

_____

_____

> Godly communication focuses on both *what* we say and *how* we say it.

❖ What does unwholesome talk include?

_____

❖ What words does Paul use to describe the more positive and preventative aspects of peacemaking?

_____

❖ Summarize the importance of encouragement and edification for peacemaking.

_____

_____

_____

❖ Think of someone right now whom you can plan to encourage/edify within the next few days. How will you do it?

_____

_____

_____

_____

_____

_____

_____

Chapter 16

Godly Communication

Godly communication is our next theme. "Words play a key role in almost every conflict. When used properly, words promote understanding and encourage agreement. When misused, they usually aggravate offenses and drive people further apart" (Sande 1992:127).

Godly communication enhances peacemaking in a proactive or preventative fashion. We must speak the truth. But the truth must be shared in love, with gentleness, wisdom and patience. We must always seek to encourage our brothers and sisters so that they are built up and our relationships stay on a positive note. Thus, Godly communication focuses on both *what* we say and *how* we say it.

Read Prov. 15:1 and answer the following questions.

❖ What is the contrast in this verse?

_____

❖ Why is "gentleness" such a key dimension of peacemaking?

_____

Read Eph. 4:15 and answer the following questions.

- What two dimensions to communication are mentioned?

  _____

- What happens if we speak truth without love or seek to love someone without truth?

  _____

  _____

Read Col. 1:28 and answer the following questions.

- What three activities describe Paul's ministry of the word?

  _____

- How did Paul proclaim, admonish and teach?

  _____

- What was the goal of Paul's ministry of the word?

  _____

Read 2 Tim. 4:2 and answer the following questions.

- What was Timothy commanded to do?

  _____

- When was he commanded to do this?

  _____

- How was he commanded to carry this out?

  _____

❖ How do "great patience" and "instruction" strengthen our relationships?

_____

_____

Read 1 Thes. 5:11-14 and answer the following questions.

❖ What are we commanded to do in v. 11?

_____

❖ How does encouragement or building others up enhance our relationships?

_____

1 Thes. 5:11-12 focuses on the relationship between leaders and the flock.

❖ What three words describe what leaders do in v. 12?

_____

❖ What three words or phrases describe how the body is to relate to its leaders?

_____

❖ List the commands in v. 14.

_____

_____

_____

Chapter Sixteen — Godly Communication

❖ What types of people does Paul mention in v. 14 and why is it important to know your audience?[21a]

_____

_____

_____

❖ Godly communication should at times be firm (admonish) and at other times sensitive (encourage, help, be patient). In your opinion, what determines when we do what?

_____

_____

_____

_____

_____

_____

_____

---

21 The Greek word translated "unruly" (NASB) or "idle" (NIV), *ataktos*, is especially interesting. It means "without rank, out of rank, disorderly. The word was primarily a military term used of the soldier who is out of step or out of rank" (Rienecker 1980:602). Thus, someone who is *ataktos* is undisciplined, insubordinate, unbridled and seeks to evade his/her responsibilities. This type of person needs to be admonished, that is, corrected through instruction and warning. The fainthearted (NASB) or timid (NIV), *oligopsuchous*, refers to someone who is discouraged, fearful and despondent. This type of person needs encouragement, not correction. And finally, the weak, *astheneis*, refers to someone who has no strength, resources or capacity to handle the situation. They need help (*antechesthe*). This word means "holding on to something, cleaving to a person. ... [T]he weak need to feel that they are not alone" (Morris 1971:101). Paul then concludes with a general exhortation to "be patient with all men." This word means, "not giving way to a short or quick temper toward those who fail, but being patient and considerate of them" (Reinecker 1980:602).

2 Tim. 2:24-25 deals with conflict, with those who have wronged us (v. 24, NASB) and those who are in opposition (v. 25). Read the passage and answer the following questions.

- ❖ List the commands in v. 24.

  _____

- ❖ How are we are to correct others, according to v. 25?

  _____

- ❖ What aspect of this passage is the most difficult for you?

  _____

  _____

- ❖ Summarize your findings from this lesson on Godly communication.

  _____

  _____

  _____

  _____

- ❖ In what ways does your communication need to improve?

  _____

  _____

  _____

  _____

Chapter 17

Wise Communication

In James 3:13-18, James describes the nature of true wisdom, first negatively then positively. Wisdom, according to James, is not primarily intellectual but relational. "The genuine Christian will always exhibit wisdom by the kind of life he lives, especially in human relationships. He will control his tongue and shun strife and controversy. The ideal of wisdom, then, is essentially ... moral rather than intellectual" (Adamson 1976:149).

James' exposition of wisdom is especially relevant in evaluating the decision-making process. How we communicate is just as important as what we communicate!

Read James 3:13-18 and answer the following questions.

❖ Notice the contrast between heavenly wisdom and earthly wisdom in this passage. List the major differences and characteristics of both.

Heavenly Wisdom   Earthly Wisdom

_____

_____

_____

_____

- ❖ Verse 17 describes eight characteristics of heavenly wisdom. Summarize the practical relevance of each of these virtues to cultivating strong relationships and peacemaking.

  Pure

  _____

  Peaceable

  _____

  Gentle ("considerate," NIV)

  _____

  Reasonable ("submissive," NIV. This word speaks of a teachable spirit, a person who is open to correction and willing to yield to new ideas or input.)

  _____

  Full of Mercy

  _____

  Full of Good Fruits

  _____

  Unwavering ("impartial," NIV)

  _____

  Without Hypocrisy ("sincere," NIV)

  _____

- ❖ What does v. 18 teach us about peacemakers? (The NIV translates v. 18 as follows: "Peacemakers who sow in peace raise a harvest of righteousness.")

  _____

Good deeds will be produced by the actions of peacemakers. Some people try to be righteous in such a way that it splits a community. The proverb instead points to goodness as the natural fruit of a peacemaker's life ... . The repetitious "sow in peace" simply underlines the fact that peacemaking is an activity producing true outward peace. *James himself is portrayed as a peacemaker in Acts 15 and 21* (Davids 1989:91, italics added).

❖ How do you need to grow in communicating wisely? Be specific!

_____

_____

_____

_____

❖ Write out below and then memorize James 3:17.

_____

_____

_____

_____

_____

_____

_____

_____

Chapter 18

Receptivity to Counsel

One important aspect of peacemaking is the idea of "receptivity" or "openness to counsel." Proverbs makes it clear that wise men and women are hungry to learn, eager for coaching and receptive to input from others. This kind of commitment greatly facilitates peace in the body.

Read Prov. 9:8 and answer the following questions:

❖ What is the contrast in this verse?

_____

❖ How does a wise man respond to reproof?

_____

Read Prov. 12:1 and answer the following questions.

❖ What is the contrast in this verse?

_____

❖ How is lack of receptivity described?

_____

Chapter Eighteen — Receptivity to Counsel

- ❖ How does this relate to peacemaking?
  _____

Read Prov. 12:15 and answer the following questions.

- ❖ What is the contrast in this verse?
  _____

- ❖ How is a wise man described?
  _____

Read Prov. 15:31-32 and answer the following questions.

- ❖ How is the receptive person described?
  _____

- ❖ How is the unreceptive person described?
  _____

- ❖ Why do you think the unreceptive person is described this way?
  _____
  _____

Read Prov. 17:10 and answer the following question.

- ❖ What does this stark contrast imply in terms of wisdom?
  _____

Read Prov. 19:20 and answer the following questions.

- ❖ What is commanded?
  _____

- ❖ What is promised to receptive people?
  _____

Read Prov. 19:25. How does a wise person respond to reproof?
_____

According to Proverbs, the wise person is receptive to counsel. S/he is willing to listen and learn from others. The whole concept of listening to others and receptivity is central to peacemaking. Remember, people who are excommunicated from the church are not expelled because of their sin. They are excommunicated because they are not willing to "listen." They are not receptive to the counsel of the brethren and are not willing to repent. As Adams notes,

> The sin that occasioned discipline may have been relatively "small" in its effects, but to *that* sin is added the *enormously* significant sin of the rejection of Christ Himself as He demands repentance through His representatives (Adams 1973:54).

❖ Summarize what Proverbs teaches about wisdom and receptivity. (For further study, see also Prov. 10:17; 11:14; 13:1,10; 24:6; 25:11,12.)

❖ How does "receptivity" enhance peacemaking?

❖ Think of a situation in which you feel you were receptive to counsel and a situation in which you were not. What made the difference? How should you have acted in order to be more receptive?

Chapter 19

God's Heart for Unity

In the next two studies, we will examine what scripture teaches about God's heart for unity in the church.

Part of following Christ is learning to love what he loves and hate what he hates. Before I planted a church in Southeast Asia, I was not very concerned about the issue of unity. Part of the reason for this was probably due to the people who talked about it in terms of the church universal. I found it overwhelming to think about churches everywhere being united. I also wasn't too impressed by the concept of unity because it is often interpreted in terms of uniformity—something I abhor! I do not want all churches to be the same. I believe in diversity!

But the issue of unity became a major concern for me when I started planting a church. Then I began to fully appreciate why God loves unity and hates division—especially because I had such a hard time maintaining unity in the church!

> The issue of unity became a major concern for me when I started planting a church.

An understanding of God's heart for unity in the church strengthens our resolve to be peacemakers and diligently work toward unity. God longs for unity and hates division. As we understand His heart for unity, we, too, will long for unity and hate division.

❖ What key points does Jesus make in his prayer for unity (John 17:21-23)?

_____

_____

Read Acts 1:14; 2:46; 4:24, 32 and answer the following questions of each passage.

❖ What facilitated unity (if mentioned)?

1:14 _____

2:46 _____

4:24 _____

4:32 _____

❖ How is the unity described?

_____

_____

_____

❖ What are the results of unity (if mentioned)?

_____

_____

Read Eph. 2:14-16 and answer the following questions.

❖ What words does Paul use to describe the unity between Jew and Gentile (and by implication all races) in this passage?

_____

_____

> ❖ What is one of the major purposes of Christ's death?
>
> _____
>
> Read Eph. 4:1-3 and answer the following questions.
>
> ❖ How does Paul describe our role in facilitating unity in the church (or on the team) in Eph. 4:3?
>
> _____

The word translated "diligent" (NASB) or "make every effort" (NIV) is the Greek word, *spoudazo*, which means to "push on with something quickly, assiduously, zealously ... it is to be used for serious effort, for taking things or people seriously ... often used as the form of urgent petition" (Kittel 1985:1069-1070).

> ❖ What is the practical relationship between Eph. 4:1-2 and 4:3?
>
> _____

According to Paul, the way we walk in a manner worthy of our calling is not to spend lots of time praying, studying the Scriptures, and witnessing, although these are important dimensions of following Christ. The worthy walk is the walk of unity in our relationships—to live in unity with our spouses, on our teams, and in our churches. And to do this we must be humble, gentle and forbearing. (Review *Peacemaking 14* on brokenness.) Moreover, we must work zealously to maintain unity in these relationships.

> ❖ Summarize why unity is important in light of all the verses studied above.
>
> _____
> _____
> _____
> _____
> _____

❖ How do you need to apply these truths about unity?

_____

_____

_____

Chapter 20

God's Hatred of Division

As we noted in our last study, part of following Christ is learning to love what he loves and hate what he hates. Jesus not only loves unity, he hates division. In fact, some of the strongest words in the Bible are used in dealing with division in the church.

> Read Prov. 6:16-19 and answer the following questions.
>
> ❖ How many of the things listed in this passage deal with disunity?
>
> _____
>
> ❖ Why do you think God hates division and dissension?
>
> _____
>
> ❖ Read Gal. 5:19-21 and answer the following question. While all of the deeds of the flesh contribute to division in the body at some level, which of these works of the flesh specifically deal with divisiveness?
>
> _____

Read Titus 3:10-11 and answer the following questions.

- ❖ What kind of people are we to excommunicate from our fellowship?

  _____

- ❖ What are the steps to excommunication in this passage?

  _____

  _____

Read Rom. 16:17-18 and answer the following questions.

- ❖ What two things are we commanded to do with divisive people in Rom. 16:17?

  _____

  _____

  _____

- ❖ How does Paul describe these divisive people in Rom. 16:18?

  _____

The Bible does not mince its words in dealing with the divisive. If we love the church as Jesus does, then we must deal biblically with divisive people and divisive behavioral patterns in the church. It is not loving or biblical to ignore division or divisive people. God hates it!

- ❖ What new things (if any) have you learned in this study?

  _____

  _____

  _____

❖ What aspects of this study do you need to apply immediately?

_____

_____

❖ What area(s) do you need to grow in?

_____

_____

_____

Chapter 21

Spiritual Warfare & Peacemaking

> Anger in a Christian is a kind of "fifth-column" available for cooperation with the enemy.

Peacemaking and spiritual warfare are intimately related. We might even say they are dangerously related! We open ourselves up to direct demonic attack when we are not in right relationship with one another. Often these open doors for the enemy are caused by what most Evangelicals consider "respectable" sin. For example, lack of forgiveness, anger, selfish ambition and jealousy are expressly described in the New Testament as handles for the evil one to invade our lives.

Note: This study focuses on only a few demonic in-roads into our lives. Many others could be mentioned. We put on the belt of truth in spiritual warfare (Eph. 6:14) because Satan is the father of lies (John 8:44). We defeat the devil with the weapons of righteousness (2 Cor. 6:7; Eph. 6:14) because he is unrighteous (1 John 3:7-10). The point is this: spiritual warfare and peacemaking are directly related to our character. To be effective in combat, we must be men and women of character.

Read 2 Cor. 2:10-11 and answer the following questions.

❖ In v. 10, Paul says he forgave an erring brother. What was the purpose of that, according to v. 11?

_____

❖ If we do not forgive someone, what can happen to us?

_____

The Greek word, *pleonektew*, means to "take advantage of" (NASB) or "outwit" (NIV). In this case, to have "an unforgiving spirit would be to grant Satan an entry where he has no right ... to yield ground to the enemy and to allow him to seize what does not belong to him" (Hughes 1975:72).

> ❖ What Satanic "schemes" do you think Paul is referring to in 2 Cor. 2:10-11?
>
> _____
>
> _____
>
> ❖ What other insights into these "schemes" do we see in Heb. 12:14-15?
>
> _____
>
> _____

The Corinthian church had rightly excommunicated a brother but had failed to restore him after he repented (2 Cor. 2:5-9). Thus, Paul exhorts them to forgive him, comfort him and reaffirm their love for him. But Paul not only exhorts them positively. He also warns them. If they do not forgive this brother, Satan can take advantage of them. Lack of forgiveness is an open door for the devil, a breeding ground for demonic bondage.

> Read Eph. 4:26-27 and answer the following questions.
>
> ❖ Is anger sin, according to this passage? (See also Mark 3:5 and James 1:19,20.)
>
> _____
>
> _____
>
> _____
>
> _____

> ❖ What three conditions does Paul add to the phrase, "be angry," and what are the implications of each one?
>
> 1. Condition: _____
>
>   Implication: _____
>
> 2. Condition: _____
>
>   Implication: _____
>
> 3. Condition: _____
>
>   Implication: _____

Verse 27 says that anger gives the devil an "opportunity" (NASB) or a "foothold" (NIV) in our lives.

> To allow anger to linger on until it grows into an enduring resentment gives opportunity to the devil, by providing him with—as it were—an ammunition-dump laid ready within the stronghold he plans to conquer. Anger in a Christian is a kind of "fifth-column" available for cooperation with the enemy (Mitton 1976:169).

> Read James 3:13-18 and answer the following questions.
>
> ❖ Notice the contrast between heavenly wisdom and earthly wisdom. How is earthly wisdom described in this passage? (See especially vs. 14-16.)
>
> _____
>
> ❖ What two types of sin are repeated in vs. 14 and 16?
>
> _____

The word "bitter jealousy" (or "envy") describes "a fierce desire to promote one's own opinion to the exclusion of others" (Reinecker 1980:735). The word "selfish ambition ... really means the vice of a leader of a party created for his own pride: It is partly ambition, partly rivalry" (Reinecker 1980:735).

- ❖ What are the three sources of wisdom that are not from above, according to James 3:15?

  _____

This wisdom is condemned in three carefully chosen adjectives, signifying respectively, godless, subhuman, and devilish … . James goes on to say that false wisdom is not only godless and subhuman but positively "devilish." The false wisdom is not merely neutral, spurious, or inadequate—but positively demonic (Adamson 1976:151-152).

- ❖ Are there areas in your life where you've given the devil a foothold? Your spouse's life? Your children's? Your team's? Your church's?

  _____

  _____

  _____

  _____

Addendum:

Peacemaking Cross-Culturally

The following is a book review of the best book available on peacemaking cross-culturally, Cross-Cultural Conflict: Building Relationships for Effective Ministry, *by Duane Elmer.*

Duane Elmer's book is an excellent introduction to the issues of peacemaking cross-culturally. He rightly points out that the Western "in your face" approach to conflict resolution will often exacerbate problems in most of the Two-Thirds World.

Part Two of the book, "Cultural Diversity and Conflict Resolution," describes biblically acceptable and culturally sensitive alternatives to the more direct Western approach to peacemaking. His discussion on the role of a mediator, storytelling, proverbs and the understanding of a shame culture is exceptional. It will also challenge many of the Western reader's cherished, ethnocentric values. This is a stimulating book—a great introduction to the complex issues of cross-cultural conflict.

Nevertheless, there are weaknesses. Elmer has rightly critiqued the Westerner's overemphasis of certain biblical values to the exclusion of other biblical values esteemed by the Two-Thirds World. But he has failed to be biblical enough. For example, Elmer equates the peacemaking procedures described by Jesus in Matthew 18:15-17 with a Western approach. But Jesus was a Middle Easterner! And since this is the word of God, Jesus expects his church to obey these steps to reconciliation in every culture.

It is true that Westerners may tend to focus too much on passages like Matthew 18 and give too great an emphasis on *what* we must say to resolve conflict. (That was my problem when I went to the field in 1984.)

> The Western "in your face" approach to conflict resolution will often exacerbate problems in most of the Two-Thirds World.

But the Bible teaches that *what* we say ***and*** *how* we say it are important. We are commanded to resolve conflict with gentleness, wisdom and patience (Gal. 6:1; Col. 1:28; Prov. 12:18, 15:2, 16:21, 25:11-12; 2 Tim. 4:2). Moreover, the use of mediation in conflict resolution, noted by Elmer as a key strategy in the Two-Thirds World, has a Biblical basis in 1 Cor. 6:1-5 and Matt. 18:16.

Elmer rightly critiques the Western approach to conflict resolution but fails to critique the Two-Thirds World. "Saving face" can be just as wrong an approach as being "in your face." Humility and the values of the kingdom of God don't always fit well with any culture—Eastern or Western. But then, Elmer's book only focuses on normal conflict in cross-cultural relationships. He doesn't promise to show us how the biblical principles of peacemaking are applied cross-culturally in a church setting. Nevertheless, his book is foundational for further study in this important area.

Conclusion

Let's conclude our study by reviewing and summarizing some of the key principles involved in peacemaking.

One Definition: Peacemaking is, resolving conflict, restoring, and building harmony in relationships.

Peacemaking:
- resolving conflict
- restoring
- building harmony in relationships.

Two Dimensions: Peacemaking has two facets, or dimensions. The reactive or restorative dimension focuses on how we can be reconciled when we are alienated. The proactive or preventative dimension focuses on building and cultivating deeper relationships through brokenness, encouragement, affirmation and Godly communication.

Three Purposes: According to the New Testament, peacemaking has three purposes: the glory of God, the welfare of the church, and the restoration of the sinner. All three of these purposes must be emphasized to have a balanced perspective and proper motivation for peacemaking.

The purposes of peacemaking:
- The glory of God.
- The welfare of the church.
- The restoration of the sinner.

We engage in peacemaking first of all to glorify God. He is glorified when unbelievers see our good deeds, and He is blasphemed when they see sin in the church (Matt. 5:16; 1 Peter 2:12; Rom. 2:24). Thus, we promote His glory and honor His name when we keep His commandments and deal with sin biblically.

Second, the goal of peacemaking is the welfare of the church. Much of Paul's teaching about the church is focused on this dimension of peacemaking. We are continually commanded to guard the purity and unity of the body (1 Cor. 5:1-13; Rom. 15:5-7, 16:17-18; Eph. 4:3; Titus 3:10-11).

The third purpose of peacemaking is restoration, to win back an erring brother or sister. Matthew 18 emphasizes this aspect of peacemaking. The parable of the lost sheep (Matt. 18:10-13) stresses the responsibility of the community to actively seek a straying brother or sister. Matt. 18:15 specifically says that the goal is to win our brother or sister. And the parable of the unmerciful servant (Matt. 18:21-35) focuses on the importance of forgiveness.

> "There is no more Godlike work to be done
> in this world than peacemaking."
> *John Broadus*

Peacemaking Applied

Part 3

PEACEMAKING APPLIED

by

Elliot Paulson

"Blessed are the peacemakers, for they shall be called sons of God." (Matt. 5:9)

Biblical peacemaking is practical, powerful, and profitable for individuals and for the community of the King. The blessing of God on peacemakers is evident, because when we reconcile people to God and to one another, we unleash a chain reaction of spiritual power that the world cannot mock and the devil cannot mimic. We have prepared *Peacemaking Applied* as a companion to Rick Love's *Peacemaking: A Study Guide* to illustrate both the benefits of peacemaking and the challenges peacemakers face. The context for our application is cross-cultural church planting teams among Muslims, but we believe the principles can be sensitively used anywhere.

In Part One, *The Explosive Power of Peacemaking*, you will read a series of examples of how biblical peacemaking released people from sin that was entangling them. You will see how loving peacemakers took risks in relationships, and how offenders responded to the Shepherd's voice calling them to repentance. You will also see how restored offenders became peacemakers themselves, multiplying the fruit of righteousness thirty, sixty, one hundred fold.

Part Two, *Responses to Questions and Objections*, addresses seventeen issues raised by those unfamiliar with or "uncomfortable" with biblical peacemaking.

All examples given are based on real people and events; some details have been changed to protect both the innocent and the guilty.

PEACEMAKING APPLIED

Part 1:
The Explosive Power of Peacemaking

Unique and irresistible spiritual power is released when the peacemaker combines reproductive teaching with a clear conscience and an exemplary life. Paul the Peacemaker knew the power of personal and relational integrity. "I also do my best to maintain always a *blameless conscience* both before God and before men" (Acts 24:16). He boldly declared, "Be imitators of me, just as I also am of Christ" (1 Cor. 11:1); "Brethren, join in *following my example*, and observe those who walk according to the pattern you have in us" (Phil. 3:17); and "The things you have learned and received and heard and *seen in me*, practice these things, and the God of peace will be with you" (Phil. 4:9). Because Paul did everything in his power to be at peace with all men (cf. Rom. 12:18), his gospel preaching and his miracle working gained an added weight that no one could stand against. He was never the subject of the proverb, "Do what the preacher *says*, not what he *does*." He could say in complete confidence, "Do what I do."

Because Paul knew what it means to fear God, he tried to persuade believers and non-believers alike to make peace with God (cf. 1 Cor. 5:1-20). In his peacemaking with believers, he risked potentially relationship-breaking reactions from Messianic Jews, from Gentile-background believers, and even from other apostles. But he was faithful to the constraining love of Christ working in and through him. The modern peacemakers described in the following discipleship chain (cf. 2 Tim. 2:2) also risked valued relationships for the love of Christ even as they strove to maintain clear consciences before man and God. They were able to say, "Do as I do."

Nathan and Daniel

Daniel was an experienced leader (TL) of a large church planting (cp) team in North Africa which was simultaneously working in four sites in a three-province area. Daniel asked his international field office to arrange for a certain cp expert to coach the team on site. The office responded with the suggestion of Nathan instead. Their reasoning was that Nathan had solid domestic cp experience, and the office wanted to recruit Nathan as a primary coach for their agency. "Thanks, but no thanks," replied Daniel. He had once attended a seminar given by Nathan, and, while impressed with Nathan's knowledge and application of Scripture, Daniel did not like Nathan's communication style or personality. But when the international office repeated their suggestion of Nathan coming to coach Daniel's team, he acquiesced.

Nathan and Daniel spent the first couple of awkward days together getting to know each other personally. As he predicted, Daniel did not naturally warm up to Nathan's personality, but he pleasantly found that Nathan was different one-on-one than in the seminar setting where he had gotten his first negative impression. Within two days, Daniel was so positively affected by Nathan's spiritual and cp experience and his knowledge of Scripture that Daniel decided to reveal to Nathan some of his most personal facts and feelings: he had almost no devotional life, he was not living up to biblical standards as a husband and father, he didn't give enough time and energy to his team, and he had little passion for his ministry to Muslims.

(Did we mention that Daniel was a respected, experienced TL with a large team in multiple cp sites?)

In Daniel's semi-deceitful heart, these revelations were both an honest confession and a falsely humble attempt to manipulate from Nathan sympathetic, pat-on-the-back praise like the comfort he had received from other older spiritual brothers when he had shared similar things with them: "What are you talking about, Daniel? Look at all you are doing for God, and in the difficult Muslim world, of all places. How many men are doing - or even *can* do - what you are doing? Lighten up. Take a break or something. I'm sure you're just overworked."

Unknown to Daniel, as he shared his mixed-motive confession, tension brewed inside Nathan. This was Nathan's first coaching trip for this agency and he desperately wanted it to be a success. He believed that Daniel was an influential leader within the agency and he wanted Daniel to give the agency's leadership a positive recommendation about him. The problem for Nathan was that he had observed that Daniel was trapped in a very specific sin. Nathan faced a hard choice. On the one hand, he could seize the opening Daniel had given him and immediately confront Daniel with his sin. If Nathan did bring revelation and if Daniel did repent, then Nathan would have won his brother and angels would have rejoiced.

However, Nathan knew from his years of peacemaking experience that there was a good possibility that Daniel might resist his admonition, and then perhaps abort the coaching trip. By rebuking Daniel now, Nathan would be risking both his newly-begun personal relationship with Daniel and a potentially long-term partnership with the agency (not to mention creating a horrible awkwardness for the remaining ten days of his planned two-week stay in Daniel's home). On the other hand, Nathan could postpone his exhortation until later in the trip. But Daniel might not give him another window like this and Nathan's bringing it up out of context could further raise the probability of Daniel's resistance.

> Of course, Nathan also had the choice of suppressing God's voice and not rebuking Daniel at all. He could simply give Daniel seasoned advice on cp, and garner a great evaluation from Daniel for the international office. But, of course, in that case he would not be obeying the Lord or loving Daniel. Nathan decided to pray and process these options in what turned out to be a sleepless, tearful night of wrestling with God. By next morning, he had chosen the way of risk-filled love and faith.

The following day, Nathan led Daniel in a study of Romans 5-7 to review Daniel's spiritual history and to see if Daniel truly was a regenerated believer. Nathan knew that such a step was necessary because not all who profess to know Christ actually do.

Daniel's testimony of conversion and his journey of faith convinced Nathan that the Holy Spirit was indeed alive in Daniel. Nathan firmly but gently looked Daniel in the eye, and softly said, "I think I know what your root sin is."

Daniel was taken aback at Nathan's calm, but direct speech. His pulse began to race and acid squirted into his stomach. With a grimace, he asked, "And what might that be?"

"Passivity. Now, passivity is not a biblical word, but James 4:17 describes it."

Red-faced, Daniel admitted that he didn't know James 4:17. His heart pumped harder.

Nathan quoted, "He who knows what to do and does not do it, to him it is sin."

Some people describe what Daniel next experienced as a truth encounter. Others call it the Holy Spirit speaking. Daniel says it felt like a bullet to the forehead: Bam! Right between the eyes. This certainly wasn't the, "Aw, you're OK; don't be so hard on yourself" response from Nathan he had been half fishing for. But in truth, Nathan's revelation was the deep desire of Daniel's redeemed heart. It was cool rain to his smoldering soul. Daniel felt like a guilt-struck thief who was relieved at finally being caught.

Daniel let out a sigh, looked down at the carpet, softly scrunched his lips and said, "Hmm. Well. Ahem. I see. Now what?"

"You need to repent," Nathan calmly said, his eyes still firm, but also full of grace.

Nathan skillfully and compassionately led Daniel through a prayer of confession for his passivity - and the related sins of self-protection and laziness - kneeling face down on the carpet. Daniel felt the refreshing comfort of the Holy Spirit and the restoration of the joy of his salvation for the first time in years.

Nathan breathed a heavy sigh of relief. In the face of risk, his choice to obey Gal. 6:1 and "gently restore one who was caught in a sin" had borne good fruit.

As an immediate application of his new-found reconciliation with God, Nathan led Daniel in repentance on his knees before Louise, his wife of twelve years. Within months, by God's grace and transforming power, Daniel began a disciplined and joyful devotional life, became more proactive in leading his family and his team, and took what were for him unprecedented and bold steps in evangelism and in mentoring Muslim Background Believer (MBB) leaders. A decade later, Louise testified that Daniel had been transformed into a "new husband," beginning with Nathan's courageous, loving admonition. Daniel's transformation continues to this day, often aided by more loving rebuke from Nathan.

Daniel and Cornell

However, soon after his initial repentance, Daniel's fleshly tendency to avoid conflict and be self-protective was tested by a younger teammate, Cornell. He had joined Daniel's team as an intern, planning to recruit and lead the first cp team on Muslim soil from an influential denomination which Daniel's agency's leadership was eager to partner with. Cornell and his wife, Susan, planned to go to a different country after their internship with Daniel's team.

Even though Daniel was more proactive and invested more time, effort, and resources in his training of Cornell than he had done with any other previous team member, he did not meet Cornell's expectations of a leader. Cornell had signed on to learn from Daniel, but not long after his arrival, he decided that Daniel was not spiritual, visionary, strategic, organized, or worshipful enough. By the end of his three-year internship, he had gathered extensive evidence of Daniel's failings, and his judgmental attitudes toward Daniel had overflowed into critical and disrespectful speech and actions.

(Did we mention that Cornell and Susan were the premier leaders of their entire denomination's hopeful new venture into the Muslim world?)

Daniel had observed these sins in Cornell, but he had sinned himself by not admonishing Cornell. In this way, Daniel broke his promise to train Cornell in character and he violated his call from God to shepherd the flock entrusted to him (1 Pet. 5:2). Fully knowing the benefit in his own life of compassionate correction brought by a loving brother, he chose not to love Cornell out of fear of facing a heated and emotional confrontation with him. By delaying his obedience to God and by withholding his love toward Cornell, Daniel allowed Cornell's sins to deepen and multiply.

When Nathan came on a coaching trip, Daniel shared his concerns about Cornell with him. Nathan led Daniel in repentance before God for his sins toward Cornell. Of course, part of Daniel's fruit in keeping with repentance was to do peacemaking with Cornell in the remaining weeks of Cornell's internship. Daniel tried several times to bring light to Cornell about his sin, but Cornell did not repent. When the time came for Daniel's final written evaluation of Cornell's internship, he penned the hardest letter he had ever written. With biblical references, Daniel stated clearly that the attitudes and actions Cornell had displayed over the years, including his not listening to gentle correction, were rooted in pride, arrogance, and lack of respect for authority. Even though Cornell's ministry *competence* (language and culture learning) was quite satisfactory, Daniel could not recommend that Cornell lead a cp team because of his *character*. Cornell's pastor agreed with Daniel's evaluation. Together, the pastor and Daniel decided that the best and most loving thing to do for Cornell was to suggest that he leave the field, and return to his home church to submit to a program of biblical character development under the authority of the home pastor.

Daniel had to deliver this message in person. Since Cornell's respect for Daniel was at an all-time low, Daniel knew the potential of his resisting correction was very high. And since Cornell and Susan were the all-star, up-front and visible leading couple in their denomination's new thrust into the Muslim world, their reaction to Daniel's admonition could torpedo his agency's budding partnership with their denomination. As predicted, Cornell and Susan reacted to Daniel's evaluation and recommendation with tears, anger and accusations.

But God is gracious and faithful. When Cornell realized he had no other practical choice at the time, he did reluctantly return to the States. After months of prayer and more revelation, Cornell miraculously began to listen to the brethren, humbled himself, and began repenting of his sins. After nine months, his transformation had progressed enough that his pastor and Daniel could recommend his return to the field. Besides repenting for his arrogance and judgment of his spiritual leaders, Cornell also had to repent of not shepherding, not caring for, and not protecting Susan, and for not living with her in an understanding way. As evidence of fruit in keeping with his repentance, while speaking in churches throughout his denomination, Daniel would say, "The reason I am home for these months is because of flaws in my own character." He also asked Daniel to be his field overseer, even though he had other excellent choices.

Today Cornell is back on a different field as a TL. Susan testifies that Cornell is greatly transformed and that he is obeying the Bible's commands to husbands. Cornell is loyal, appreciative, submissive and respectful to his peers and authorities, including Daniel. His ministry competence has increased along with the quality of his character. And he has become a peacemaker in his own right, as illustrated by his relationship with North African MBBs Omar and his wife, Aisha.

Cornell and Omar

Omar had once made good money working in a leather factory, but his boss had fired him after he was arrested for taking part in political demonstrations. Before he met Cornell, he had been unemployed for over a year, embarrassingly having to live off of loans and favors from family and friends. Aisha had never worked outside the home. She was illiterate and had two pre-school children. Susan visited Aisha regularly, reading the Bible to her and mentoring her in child rearing. Susan had three children of her own. Her oldest was 10 years older than Aisha's firstborn.

After many months of weekly visiting and studying the Scriptures, both Omar and Aisha placed their trust in Christ. Omar only had an elementary school education, but used his sharp mind to memorize Bible verses quickly and accurately. He was also a bold evangelist among his relatives and friends. He even suggested that he and Cornell go on an evangelistic tour of his home region, where there were no foreign workers and only a handful of known MBBs. For close to a year, the Omars hosted a weekly discussion group for their relatives and friends in their simple home. Cornell and Susan taught the Omars to worship the Messiah with forms that suited their cultural context. One cousin of Omar's came to Christ. An acquaintance of Omar's, the head of a significant ethnic cultural association, made great strides towards belief in the Messiah during a weekly seekers' Bible study. The Cornells saw the Omars and these first fruits of their evangelism as the seedlings of a church movement whose testimony of the Messiah's love would spread into a vast network of close-knit relatives and friends.

From the time they met, Cornell had tried all of his contacts in the city to find Omar a full-time job, with no success. Omar had found a few short-term, odd jobs on his own. But they found nothing permanent. Cornell used this time to disciple Omar in praying and trusting God to provide for him and his family, but he still expected and encouraged Omar to search for work. By drinking thousands of late-night glasses of tea and inhaling second-hand smoke from an equal number of cigarettes, Cornell proved his commitment to and care for Omar.

Even before he believed in the Messiah, Omar had demonstrated that he was not a typical husband of his culture. Aisha had admitted to him that she had been unfaithful to him more than once, but unlike the cultural norm would expect, Omar neither banished Aisha nor killed her. Though it wasn't easy for him to face the daily shame of neighbors and relatives who gossiped about what a weak man he was, he was heroic in his self-righteous refusal to "clean his honor" by getting revenge from his wife and her adulterous partners. Of course, now that he believed in the Messiah, he knew he could never harm her, and had to keep forgiving her. But the ever-nagging stress of never knowing which men he could trust around Aisha – including neighbors and relatives – took its emotional and physical toll on him. Aisha had also confessed her unfaithfulness to Susan and Cornell. Susan and Cornell kept this in mind when discipling the Omars about their marriage.

But a phone call late one hot summer night changed everything. Aisha informed a shocked Susan that she had borrowed money for a bus ticket from a neighbor, and had escaped with the kids to her parents' home, twelve hours away. She wanted to divorce Omar. He had beaten her, but this wasn't her real reason for fleeing. Aisha now claimed that Omar had forced her to confess all the instances of her unfaithfulness to him, and he was constantly pressuring her to confess more. For the first time, she denied to Susan that she had ever committed adultery. She was finally fed up with Omar's continual suspicions and threats to beat more confessions out of her.

Susan and Cornell were confused and crushed. They had never seen such an attitude in the normally meek and quiet Aisha. Could Aisha actually be telling the truth now? Cornell and Susan knew that Aisha's family had always verbally abused her and made her life miserable. What would she have to gain now by lying to Omar, Cornell, and Susan and then seeking refuge with her family? On the other hand, Omar was so sincere and growing in Christ, how could he have so boldly hidden this lie from them?

Cornell immediately called Omar over to their house to talk and pray. Omar said that Aisha had left him a cassette tape renouncing her confessions, confronting him with his anger and violence, and listing her conditions for her return. When Cornell pressed him, Omar admitted that he had indeed physically forced those confessions from Aisha.

(Did we mention that Cornell and Susan viewed Omar and Aisha as the keys to a whole church movement among their close-knit network of friends and relatives?)

Now Cornell and Susan felt like utter and complete failures. How could they have missed the truth of this hugely important issue in the Omars' marriage?

Cornell tried to convince Omar that the only thing for him to do was to swallow his pride, confess and repent of his beatings of Aisha, promise to trust and take care of her, and to go get her. He consented.

Aisha accepted Omar's repentance for beating her, forgave him, and returned home with the condition that if Omar ever verbally or physically threatened her again, she would immediately call Cornell and Susan, day or night.

In the weeks ahead, Cornell worked with Omar specifically on his role as a Messiah-following husband, in addition to their normal times of discipleship and weekly seekers' meetings. As Aisha shared more of her feelings with Susan and Susan brought the Word of God to meet her needs, Aisha's pure, simple faith grew.

But seven months later, Aisha called Susan with another shock. Omar's suspicions of her had come back; indeed they had intensified and multiplied. She said he had hit her twice in two weeks to get two more confessions out of her. She had left him again.

In God's sovereignty, Daniel was planning a visit within a few days, so when Cornell called Daniel with the news, they decided to do peacemaking with Omar together. Omar agreed with Cornell's idea to meet with Daniel, whom he had met several times on previous visits and recognized as an older spiritual brother to Cornell.

Daniel, Cornell, and Omar

For five hours one afternoon sitting in Cornell's office, Daniel and Cornell listened to Omar's life story. He had been stigmatized as a child because he was thought to be illegitimate. When he left his village for the opportunities of the big city, he faced persecution because of his minority ethnic background. His life had been nothing but struggle. However, he was grateful for the Lord's saving him and for Cornell's invaluable and seemingly inexhaustible investment in his life. Yet, he felt trapped in circumstances beyond his control. The bad economy and social prejudice kept him from finding a permanent job, and his relatives were of almost no help. What help they gave only made him more in their debt. He loved his wife, and though he wanted to trust her with all his heart, he simply could not trust her around any other man, including his relatives. He couldn't walk down the street without feeling that neighborhood men were smirking and mocking him for his weakness as a man unable to control his roaming wife. Even one of his closest friends wouldn't look him in the eye and had been avoiding him lately, which Omar took as a sure sign that he, too, had violated Omar's honor by having sex with Aisha. This was the latest confession she had made.

Omar passionately explained that he forgave Aisha, but he could not trust her, no matter how much he tried. He wanted God's help to trust her. But how could he, when she even confessed to her infidelity?

When Daniel questioned the validity of Aisha's so-called confessions, Omar responded, "Older brother Daniel, you know North African culture. No one admits to a sin or crime here when simply confronted verbally. I *had* to convince her to confess. You be the judge. One the one hand, you've heard the evidence I have given. On the other, you have her denial."

Daniel responded, "Well, Omar, I appreciate your asking me to be the judge here. And since you did, I must say that when I look at things objectively, I see that all of your so-called evidence for her adultery is at best circumstantial. Do you have any solid proof that Aisha ever committed adultery?"

"No, I don't. But if you were me, wouldn't it look that way to you?"

"It might, *if* I had previously convinced myself that my wife was by nature unfaithful and that every man she ever meets is a probable partner of hers. But nothing you have said would lead me to that conclusion unless I already thought that way."

Omar protested, "Well, what about her confessions?"

"Omar, remember that you asked me to be the judge. As you admitted, I do know the so-called justice system here. You're right. No one here admits guilt until they've been beaten by the police, and everyone signs a confession after they have been beaten. But good judges never allow confessions in court because the accused always swears to the judge that he confessed to the police under duress. The good judges believe the accused because they also know how the police get confessions."

Omar sheepishly smiled in agreement. He realized he had been exposed by his own analogy.

Daniel went on. "Omar, let's not talk about earthly judges. Let's look at your situation from God's kingdom point of view. You know that as the husband, God holds you responsible for your family, and He will judge you according to biblical standards for husbands. I know Cornell has been studying the biblical commands to husbands with you, so I won't repeat them here. But, Omar, when God asks you - He's actually asking you right now - how your beating Aisha shows that you cherish her, protect her, love her, and give yourself up for her as Christ loved the church, what can you say? She is God's precious gift to you. How does God feel about the way you have been caring for his precious gift? You've talked about your honor to us for five straight hours. As a father, put yourself in God's place. What about *His* honor? How do you think God feels about your treatment of His daughter, Aisha, whose care he entrusted you with? And by the way, I'll ask you the question that I ask myself and every husband I work with, *Just who do you think you are anyway, that you deserve this wonderful woman God has given you?*

"Now I want you to listen carefully and consider something that will be very radical and difficult for you. Meditate on the possibility that you have been totally wrong in your beliefs about Aisha. Ask God to reveal to you whether the following possible scenario is true: that because of your prejudiced, unfounded belief that Aisha is inherently adulterous, you have been suspicious of her, you have looked for any possible sign of her cheating on you, that you have seen every man around her as a potential partner for her, that you have wrongly believed that she indeed committed adultery with relatives and neighbors. And so believing, you beat confessions out of this poor, delicate gift of God. And, hypocritically, claiming to be so concerned for what men think of you, you never even confronted the men you accused in your heart.

"You then self-righteously thought that your keeping Aisha as your wife and not divorcing her (or even killing her, as the culture would allow), and your enduring the shame she has brought on your honor were grand acts of spiritual maturity and personal sacrifice.

"If what I am asking you to consider is right, think of the evil results of your false belief: you have sinned against God, against your wife, against your kids, against your relatives and neighbors; you have caused gossip and strife in your extended family, and ruined Aisha's reputation. And, you have trapped yourself in a cycle of fear and anger.

"Don't let me put words into your mouth. I just want you to consider these possibilities with an honest mind and a clear heart."

Omar was silent for some minutes. Then he said, "Older brother Daniel, I've thought about what you just said. I've come to the conclusion that you are absolutely right. I have been wrong in my belief about Aisha, and because of my wrong belief, I terribly hurt and sinned against the precious gift God gave me, I have slandered her, my neighbors, and my relatives, and I have been the cause of all of our broken relationships. I let myself believe a lie, and that lie was the source of all the other sins I committed. I accept full responsibility, and am ready to repent."

The three men knelt and buried their faces in the back of their hands on the floor. Omar confessed his wrong belief about Aisha and how that root sin led to his other sins against God, Aisha, his relatives, and neighbors. Without prompting, he also confessed how his deceit caused so much grief and trouble for Cornell and Susan. Daniel and Cornell thanked God for Omar's repentance, and prayed for more humility and therefore more grace for him. Afterwards, Daniel declared Omar forgiven for what he had confessed, according to 1 John 1:9.

The three then discussed how Omar would produce fruit in keeping with this repentance. The first, they agreed, would be for him to confess all of these root sins to Aisha, with Cornell and Susan present. Omar would also pray and work with Cornell to find appropriate times and contexts in which to repent to the relatives and friends he had slandered.

A few days later Omar repented of his root sins to Aisha, with Cornell and Susan as witnesses. Months later, Aisha testified that Omar had been transformed into a more godly husband. She says she feels more loved, cared for, and cherished by him. Even Omar and Aisha's children began growing in their own trust of both their earthly and Heavenly Fathers, and saw miraculous answers to their simple prayers. Anyone who knows male-dominated cultures like theirs can see that Omar's change is nothing short of a miracle.

Three months after his repentance, the Lord provided a steady job for Omar, and the influential head of their ethnic cultural association came into the Kingdom.

(Did we mention that Cornell and Susan see Omar and Aisha as keys to a church movement among their tight-knit network of relatives and friends?)

From Nathan to Daniel to Cornell to Omar, you have seen the multiplying power of peacemaking through a single chain of discipleship between generations and across cultures. (We could give many, many more examples.) Note that each peacemaker, at each step of the way, risked relationships, personal rejection, and potential ministry "success" to obey the law of love and do unto others as they would have others do unto them. They were emboldened in their peacemaking not only because they were commanded to do it by Scripture, but also because they could say with a clear conscience, "God opposes the proud, but gives grace to the humble. Do as I do, and repent when you receive revelation of sin from the brethren." *It is sobering to ponder what would have happened if, starting with Nathan, any of these men had disobeyed God's command to love through peacemaking.*

It also gives one pause to realize that *at any step* along the way, *any* offender described here *could have* resisted his brothers' peacemaking, *could have* slid deeper into his selfish sin, and could have terminated the ever-lengthening chain of transformation. But, by the grace of God given to them, these offenders did repent. And they brought forth fruits of righteousness in keeping with their repentance, restoring relationships with God and with all men and women.

PEACEMAKING APPLIED

Part 2:
Responses to Questions and Objections

This is a collection of practical notes from our experience in applying peacemaking to cross-cultural church planting (cp) team relationships and discipling Muslim Background Believers in Jesus (MBBs). *However, keeping that context in mind, we believe the principles can be sensitively applied to any cultural setting.* We have chosen to present these notes in the form of responses to some of the questions and criticisms we have encountered from cp team members and sending churches. These are the challenges we answer:

1. *"Repentance doesn't solve everything."*
2. *"Your peacemaking model is too simplistic."*
3. *"You call personality differences sin."*
4. *"There was more conflict after you tried peacemaking than there was before."*
5. *"Direct confrontation of sin is an American practice."*
6. *"Encouraging someone to admit sin to other people is inappropriate in 'shame' cultures."*
7. *"Doesn't your peacemaking go too far, too deep, too soon?"*
8. *"You should wait to rebuke until the offender is ready to hear your correction."*
9. *"Where is grace in your peacemaking?"*

10. *"We're not opposed to peacemaking, we're opposed to the way you do it."*
11. *"We do not have to rebuke sin in mature believers; we can trust God to speak to them in His time."*
12. *"You should not judge motives."*
13. *"Your peacemaking causes hurt feelings."*
14. *"You should not exhort anyone to be confronted by a peacemaker whom he fears."*
15. *"Shouldn't you make use of psychological concepts while peacemaking?"*
16. *"You try to trap people with their own words."*
17. *"Your peacemaking is too authoritarian."*

ASSUMPTION

We assume the reader is familiar with Rick Love's *Peacemaking: A Study Guide*. (Occasional references will be made to Dick Scoggins' *Principles for the Healing of Souls / Transformational Ministry* teachings, but having read them is not essential for understanding the following material.) Other than a brief review of terms, we will try not to repeat these teachings, but we will make occasional references to them.

ESSENTIAL TERMS DEFINED

Peacemaking

The word peacemaking means to make peace where peace is not. Specifically, we mean making peace between man and God, and between man and man. Where there is no conflict, peacemaking is not needed. All conflict between man and God is the result of sin, and sin is the primary source of conflict between people. Rick uses the term peacemaking as a synonym for both reconciliation and church discipline. We will do the same.

Sin

Any word, attitude, or action which is contrary to what God has commanded believers to do or be. This means doing something we are not supposed to do (a sin of commission) and not doing what we are supposed to do (a sin of omission). See Mark 12:28-31, John 14:21, Matt. 7:12, Jas. 4:17.

Offended

The person who has actually been sinned against, or, at the beginning of peacemaking, believes he has been sinned against.

Offender

The person who has sinned, or, at the beginning of peacemaking, is believed to have sinned. He may have sinned against God without obvious implications for other people, or his sin may have also been against another person(s). A resistant offender willfully tries to block the peacemaking process at some point.

Peacemaker

Whoever initiates or pursues the peacemaking process besides the offender and the offended (Matt. 18:15-17, Gal. 6:1). When the offender (Matt. 5:23-24) or the offended (Matt. 18:15) initiate peacemaking, they are also called peacemakers.

Advocate

A person(s) called in by an offender to support him in his resistance to peacemaking efforts. This person could be a spouse, a teammate, a home church pastor/elder, a coach not directly related to the sending agency, an expatriate (expat) worker, another MBB, etc.

A BRIEF REVIEW OF PEACEMAKING

When on trial before King Agrippa, the apostle Paul summarized God's call on his life like this:

> "I am sending you to open their eyes so that they may turn from darkness to light and from the dominion of Satan to God, that they might receive forgiveness of sins and an inheritance among those who have been sanctified by faith in Me" (Acts 26:17-18). Paul then explained how he lived out that call: "So King Agrippa, I did not prove disobedient to the heavenly vision, but kept declaring to those of Damascus first, and also at Jerusalem and then throughout all the region of Judea, and even to the Gentiles, that they should repent and turn to God, performing deeds appropriate to repentance" (Acts 26:19-20).

From these verses, we see that Paul's ministry had three elements:

Revelation: " I am sending you to open their eyes"

Repentance: "that they should repent and turn to God"

Righteousness: "performing deeds appropriate to repentance"

This pattern concerns the break in relationship between men and God. The healing of relationships between people follows the same cycle. When one person commits a biblical sin against another, their relationship is broken (as is the offender's relationship with God, cf. Ps. 51:3). The relationship is reconciled and restored when the offender sees his sin, repents of it before God and the offended, and brings forth righteous fruits in keeping with that repentance, and when the offended forgives the offender. The goal of peacemaking is to bring both the offender and the offended through this process.

The essential steps in the peacemaking process include:

1a. An offender receives revelation that he has offended someone, and goes to that person to reconcile. (Matt. 5:23-24)

OR

1b. An offended person confronts an offender one-to-one, and if necessary, brings others into the matter. (Matt. 18:15-17)

AND

2. The offended grants forgiveness to the repentant offender in a covenant of forgiveness. The offense is covered in the blood of Christ, and the relationship is restored.

AN APOLOGETIC FOR PEACEMAKING

Before we address criticisms and challenges we have faced, we want to communicate our commitment to, and enthusiasm for, peacemaking. It is not an optional, but essential, part of cp. For, at every cp phase, our calling is to reconcile men to God and to each other (2 Cor. 5:17-20). MBB churches or cp teams cannot be healthy or biblical without peacemaking.

Our enthusiasm for peacemaking comes from the fact that we have been personally transformed into Christ's image from one stage of glory to another (2 Cor. 3:18) when the brethren have loved us enough to practice peacemaking on us. We have also witnessed the joy of release from the power of sin, and glory to God given by MBBs and expat cp team members who have responded positively.

In short, we do peacemaking because God commands it and we have seen its countless benefits in ourselves, in our churches, and in our ministry to Team Leaders (TLs), Team Members (TMs), and MBBs.

Our treatment of the challenges we have faced in peacemaking which follows is meant to encourage, not discourage you. We want you to know that even though peacemaking can be wearying, frustrating, and time consuming, it is worth the effort. No one should be surprised by its difficulties, since peacemaking confronts the human will and sinful flesh while at the same time it attacks the enemy in the most crucial battlefield, the human heart. We often challenge strongholds of sin in believers that have never been threatened before, and sometimes neither the offender nor the devil give in to the Holy Spirit without a fight. Some offenders never give in at all, others only partially. But those who do yield to God with a broken and contrite heart find new joy, faith, power, and confidence in ministry.

CONFESSIONS OF PEACEMAKERS

We have one more subject to cover before we address criticisms to our peacemaking. We must confess that we have made many mistakes, and have even sinned, while attempting to make peace. We are far from perfect. We need and are committed to receiving coaching and upgrading in this area, just as we need continual upgrading in all other areas of cp.

We confess that we have not shown Christ's love at all times to all parties in peacemaking. A.W. Tozer, widely known as the "20th century prophet," was never timid when it came to reconciling men to God and to each other. But he was also aware of the dangers of over-enthusiasm in any spiritual venture:

> "There are areas in our lives where in our effort to be right we may go wrong, so wrong as to lead to spiritual deformity. To be specific let me name a few:
>
> 1. When in our determination to be bold we become brazen.
> 2. When in our desire to be frank we become rude.
> 3. When in our effort to be watchful we become suspicious."
>
> *(That Incredible Christian)*

We admit that at times, we have become brazen, rude, and suspicious in our peacemaking. In addition, we have not been as skilled as we should be. We have not known how to identify specific root sins, and we have not known how to listen and speak accurately and compassionately. We have moved the process along too slowly or too quickly. We have chosen meekness when we should have taken authority. We have spoken sternly when we should have comforted with compassion.

In short, we are cracked, common vessels who are simply trying to obey our Master's command to make peace as an essential part of the cp task. We often fail and sin in peacemaking, just as we often fail and sin in evangelism and discipleship. But we repent, are renewed, and we do not let our weaknesses hinder our calling as peacemakers for Christ.

CHALLENGES AGAINST PEACEMAKING

We expect that if you do peacemaking, you will (or have) run into the following challenges to peacemaking, just as we have. Each topic heading is an actual quote from an MBB or expat offender or their advocates.

1. "Repentance doesn't solve everything."

In the midst of a peacemaking effort by a TL toward a TM couple, the TM couple's home pastor told them, "Repentance doesn't solve everything." The pastor was referring to our attempts to persuade the couple to repent of various sins in their lives, and this couple appealed to their home pastor for rationale to abort our peacemaking. The pastor supported them, and he instructed them and us to stop the peacemaking process. While claiming repentance doesn't solve everything, they purposely destroyed their chance to discover exactly how much repentance *could have* solved.

Peacemaking fails only when one or more parties refuse revelation, refuse to repent, refuse to do appropriate acts of righteousness after repentance, or refuse to forgive. We have not seen any sin or interpersonal conflict that has not been resolved among believers when all parties involved show godly humility, repentance (2 Cor. 7:10), forgiveness (Matt. 6:15), and bring forth fruits in keeping with repentance (Matt. 3:8).

Even if we grant the possibility that repentance doesn't "solve everything," we are still fully convinced that without repentance no broken relationship between man and man or man and God will ever be totally reconciled. Repentance may not be the *end* of the process (actually bringing forth fruits of righteousness is), but it must be *in* the process.

2. "Your peacemaking model is too simplistic."

We agree that our model of peacemaking is not complicated: we reveal sin, then urge repentance, forgiveness, acts of righteousness, and reconciliation. *Some characterize our peacemaking methods as beating a person on the head with a Bible until he repents of something, without our listening to him or caring about his perspective, his feelings, and his other real and perceived problems. Nothing could be farther from the truth.* The whole biblical process we go through requires each person involved in a conflict to search his heart: the offender (and his advocate(s)), the offended, and the peacemaker. It takes discernment, wisdom, humility, patience, courage, trust, contriteness, and faith. Simple, maybe. Simplistic, no.

Let us illustrate how our simple method is applied in different circumstances by looking at 1 Thess. 5:14. "We urge you, brethren, admonish the unruly, encourage the fainthearted, help the weak, be patient with everyone." Paul commands Timothy to treat three types of people according to their spiritual and emotional states. He gives Timothy clear, concise instruction on how to act toward each one. First are the idle or unruly. The Greek word here, *ataktos*, carries the connotation of being out of line or insubordinate. These brethren need to be warned or admonished, that is, actively confronted and corrected for their sin. The fainthearted or timid need to be encouraged and built up (the Greek word *oligopsuchos* means despondent or literally, "small souled"). And thirdly, the weak (*asthenes*: without strength, feeble) should be helped.

At first glance, this command seems easy to obey. Paul describes three types of people, and gives three ways to react to them. It is simple. If a brother is out of line, we correct him. If a sister is timid, we encourage her. If a brother is weak, we help him.

If on our first attempt to do these things our spiritual sibling is saved from his situation, we rejoice. But often our initial warnings, encouragement, and help do not significantly improve the brother's situation. In that case, the law of love implores us to go further. For example, if a sinning brother does not listen to our first rebuke, we are obligated to proceed on in the peacemaking process. If a fainthearted sister is not encouraged by our first efforts, we must seek to find a solution at the source of her discouragement. If a weak brother is not strengthened by our initial help, he may need further training in righteousness to become strong. It is at these times that discernment, sensitivity, and wisdom are necessary.

We have often found that a person is not *just* unruly, not *just* timid, or not *just* weak at any given time. These traits are often found in combination; one can even cause another. Believers often step out of line because they are small of spirit or fainthearted. They end up sinning because they don't have the courage to follow what they know to be right.

For example, take the apostle Peter's sin of denying the Lord. His sin of lying was probably rooted in the fear of man. Or, in the words of 1 Thess. 5:14, Peter's faintheartedness caused him to be unruly. According to this verse, a fainthearted Peter should be strengthened and an unruly Peter should be admonished. But which should happen first? Where should a TL start if he has a team member or an MBB disciple like Peter? Some TLs, making encouragement the priority, would ignore that Peter sinned, convinced that Peter's timidity was the cause of his betrayal. They would try to strengthen Peter in the Lord and hope that a newly-emboldened Peter would not sin again. Other TLs would try to strengthen Peter first, but would also make it a point to confront him about his sin later. Still other TLs would be convinced that a Peter who was first forgiven and freed from the weight of his sin would then more readily benefit from words of encouragement. These TLs would first admonish Peter's sin, and then lead him to repentance and renewal and encouragement. Both the second and third approaches fit into our "simplistic" model of peacemaking. We would *both* encourage the fainthearted Peter *and* admonish the unruly Peter, determining the order based on discernment and the need of the moment.

How did the Master Peacemaker deal with the fainthearted and unruly Peter? Immediately after the third time Peter denied knowing Jesus, "The Lord turned and looked straight at Peter. Then Peter remembered the word the Lord had spoken to him: 'Before the rooster crows today, you will disown me three times.' And he went outside and wept bitterly" (Luke 22:60-62).

It is difficult to say if the Lord's gaze into Peter's eyes was encouragement for his timidity or admonishment for his sin. But we do know that this one look from Jesus made Peter "weep bitterly." This was godly sorrow which led Peter to repentance, to forgiveness, and then on to strength of heart.

We have said that Peter was disobedient because he was fainthearted. There is another connection between two problems of people described in 1 Thess. 5:14. Sometimes people become spiritually weak because they have sinned. The Psalmist knew full well that it was his own unconfessed sin that caused his weakness: "When I kept silent about my sin, my body wasted away through my groaning all day long. For day and night Your hand was heavy upon me; my vitality was drained away as with the fever heat of summer" (Ps. 32:3-4). The Psalmist's situation reminds us of TLs, TMs, and MBBs who have been severely weakened. Paul tells Timothy to "help the weak." Our peacemaking method helps us discover whether the source of the weak one's suffering is his own sin or something else. *We certainly do not believe that all weakness is caused by sin*, but if it is, as in the case of the Psalmist, the absolute best help we can offer the weakened sinner is to lead him to the refreshing fountain of Jesus' blood and the rest found at His cross. In a word, repentance provides him with the most strength. The Psalmist confirms the joyous vigor he received from being honest about his sin, repenting and being forgiven: "How blessed is he whose transgression is forgiven, whose sin is covered! How blessed is the man to whom the LORD does not impute iniquity, and in whose spirit there is no deceit!" (Ps. 32:1-2).

"Admonish the unruly, encourage the fainthearted, help the weak, be patient with everyone." We believe that in our "simplistic" peacemaking model, we strive to be patient with the unruly, the fainthearted, the weak — everyone. Yet our patience, tolerance, and kindness toward the unruly, fainthearted, and weak is not without aim, just as the Lord's kindness, tolerance and patience is not without purpose: "Or do you think lightly of the riches of His kindness and tolerance and patience, not knowing that the kindness of God leads you to repentance?" (Rom. 2:4).

3. "You call personality differences sin."

Months after our peacemaking efforts were aborted by a pastor calling a team member home to get away from an "unhealthy and harsh team environment," an elder of that church told us, "The problem was that you called personality differences sin." The elder had only heard the input of his church member, which is a common problem that can derail peacemaking (Prov. 18:17).

We responded to the elder in this way: "Sir, we acknowledge that there are personality differences between your church member and his team leader. However, you need to know that your team member committed biblical sins and would not repent of them." We described the team member's words and actions of the previous few months, and then identified those with biblical sins, and asked him, "Sir, now are these personality traits or sins?" The elder had no further comment.

We concede that it can be difficult for persons of radically different natural personalities to work in a close environment like a cross-cultural cp team. What we are warning against is a tendency for disgruntled TLs or TMs (or MBBs) who have gotten to know and accept each other enough to sign an agreement to work together (or Memorandum of Understanding or church membership covenant) to later unilaterally break that covenant, citing "personality differences." This is almost always an evasion of the real issues which strained the relationship. The real issues are almost always sin on one or both parts.

Recognizing personality and spiritual gifting in peacemakers, offenders, and the offended is essential to success in peacemaking. It is precisely because we recognize we have such varied personalities that we need to continually upgrade our skills of peacemaking, and discern how to help each personality type in the process of transformation. In Rick Love's manual, he and Dick Scoggins describe how three kinds of people respond to conflict. The Conflict Exposer, or Prophet's, message to others is, "Walk in the light!" The Conflict Controller, or Pastor's, message is, "Walk in wisdom!" The Conflict Avoider, or Mercy Shower's, message is, "Walk in grace!" Let's look at these in terms of both personality and spiritual gifting.

Take just two major temperament differences. Some people tend to approach people and events from a thinking, or cognitive point of view. A "thinker's" approach to life, and therefore conflict, is to look primarily at facts, truth, and principles. He will tend to be a Conflict Exposer or Conflict Controller. By contrast, some people lean toward considering others' feelings before all else. A "feeler" is primarily concerned with the emotions and potential hurt of those involved, and will often be a Conflict Avoider. *Thinkers* need to learn how to appropriately consider *feelings* and *emotions* during conflict, and *feelers* need to learn how to appropriately consider *facts* and *truth*.

We have noticed that there is often a correspondence between spiritual gifts and natural responses to conflict. Peacemakers with gifts of mercy, helps, and compassion can tend to be Conflict Avoiders. Peacemakers with gifts of prophecy, wisdom, teaching, and discernment can tend to be Conflict Exposers or Conflict Controllers.

Let us look at two more major personality differences: introversion and extroversion. Neither characteristic is necessarily good or bad in itself, but each has its fleshly tendency to sin. Natural introverts often are so quiet and reserved that they need to be urged to share their true thoughts and feelings (Eph. 4:25). Extroverts are often so verbal that they dominate conversations and meetings. They need to learn to be quiet so others can speak (Jas. 1:19). Each personality type's flesh will tend to sin in a different way, and the peacemaker needs to learn how to bring revelation to each person according to the need of the moment. In the case of an introvert who does not speak even when it is his time and responsibility to do so, his silence may be a sin. On the other hand, an extrovert who continually shares his thoughts and feelings without considering others may be sinning. Each natural personality type needs to learn to "consider others more important than themselves" (Phil. 2:3) in a different way.

It is important for a peacemaker to know his own personality and gifts, and their corresponding strengths and weaknesses. He must also learn the personality and gifts of the offender, the offended, and the other peacemakers with whom he is doing peacemaking. He must not allow significant personality differences, various communication styles, or the misuse of spiritual gifts to prevent revelation, repentance, acts of righteousness, and forgiveness. All Christians are called to evangelize, but not all have the gift of evangelism. In the same way, all peacemakers, whatever their personal gifts are, must prophesy, use wisdom, and practice mercy, discernment, and compassion according to the need of the moment. A skilled peacemaker's message to every person involved will be, "Walk in the light and walk in wisdom and walk in grace!"

4. "There was more conflict after you tried peacemaking than there was before."

Peace*makers* are not peace*keepers*. Peace*makers* bring peace where there is none. Peace*keepers* assume that there is peace as long as there is no open fighting, and try to keep the status quo. In our particular adopted Muslim culture, most disagreements between people end up in a separated relationship. Neither party will speak to each other. They will go out of their way to avoid each other. There is "peace" in the sense that they are not actively fighting, but there is no true peace because they are inwardly at war with each other. The cultural norm is for peacekeepers to try to get the parties together but act as if nothing has happened, without the offended and offender discussing the issues, and without repentance and forgiveness. These local peacekeepers want everyone to feel good, be happy, and avoid conflict at all costs. By contrast, a biblical peacemaker (often in violation of local cultural norms!) tries to bring the offended and offender face to face for appropriate confession of sin and forgiveness. This can *look* like the peacemaker is initiating conflict, but it is really the first step on the path to true peace.

On cp teams and in MBB churches, we often see how peace*keepers* (or conflict avoiders) let a person's sin and the bad fruit of broken relationships grow and grow until the devil chooses to use the situation for his advantage. It is much better for a peacemaker to initiate a confrontation too early than too late.

Through what may be no fault of their own, peacemakers can also be enemy makers. Resistant offenders and their advocates usually vilify and verbally attack the peacemaker. We have made many enemies because we make peace with authority and persuasion, even though we are also gentle, patient, humble, and compassionate. After a one-on-one session over a team member's sins of deception and rebellion against his team leader and God, we asked the team member, "Now we know that we have said some very hard things to you today. For our own upgrading we'd like your opinion if we have been gentle or not." The team member replied, "I must admit that you were gentle." But he didn't repent. Based on his unilateral reporting to his sending church, the church notified us that we were to cease all contact with the team member, and the church accused us of being harsh, abusive, and without grace in our treatment of him, even though the church never directly discussed with us the 112 pages of email and meeting notes of the case we provided.

The sad fact is that many churches (we have had difficulties with churches in at least four countries so far) simply do not understand and/or believe in peacemaking. We know of churches that no longer recommend certain sending agencies because those agencies have practiced peacemaking with their members and they have resisted. One sending agency national director summarizes the problem: "We are suffering with churches that have never done church discipline."

Our peacemaking with MBBs and with workers outside of our own agency has tarnished our reputation among some. You can see the potential for gossip and slander when expats who do not understand or believe in peacemaking become advocates for unrepentant MBBs or other expat workers. But those expats and MBBs who listen and respond to peacemaking call us blessed.

Sometimes a peacemaker creates enemies without even confronting directly, but simply by exposing sin in other ways. We were asked by a TL to visit him on the field and to answer specific questions relating to his ministry. When we asked informational questions about these areas, the TL became increasingly defensive and angry. He then rejected the advice we gave him and practical help we offered in all areas. Our questions had exposed that the TL was not genuinely interested in receiving true help and upgrading to improve his situation for the long term. After our trip, we received an email from the TL with a page and a half of accusations against us: We hadn't listened to him, we weren't understanding, we only criticised, we gave no encouragement, we showed no compassion or grace. This was his response to honest questions about his ministry; we hadn't even rebuked him for any specific sins!

Let it be clearly understood that we do not believe that we should admonish every "little" sin the first time we see it in our brother, especially if it is directed toward us personally. Proverbs 19:11 instructs us: "A man's wisdom gives him patience; it is to his glory to overlook an offence." (NIV) *Our concern here is the rebuke of a man's sins that affect his testimony and his witness as an ambassador for Christ.*

We know of no godly peacemaker who enjoys the process of rebuking and correcting sin in others. If someone enjoys confrontation, then he is simply not a peacemaker. A godly person only pursues peacemaking under the conviction that it is in the best interest of the offender (1 Cor. 14:3). A true peacemaker normally rebukes only after praying that the offender will be convicted by his own conscience, or by the Word, or by the Holy Spirit. When it is evident that the offender needs to be rebuked, the peacemaker prays, "Lord, may this cup pass from me." If the Lord does not take the cup away, the peacemaker clears the logs out of his own eyes, and brings rebuke with the godly traits of humility, patience, gentleness, and compassion. Now, it is not *these* particular godly characteristics which create enemies for a peacemaker; it is his *other* godly traits that create enemies. For, a godly peacemaker rebukes with authority from God himself (Titus 2:15). He also speaks with persuasion, begging the offender to be reconciled with God (2 Cor. 5:11, 20).

It is certainly not uplifting, edifying, or encouraging to face the wrath of individuals and churches who refuse admonition, but let us not be discouraged from peacemaking because we have made enemies while trying to make peace. After all, the Bible warns us: "He who corrects a scoffer gets dishonor for himself, and he who reproves a wicked man gets insults for himself" (Prov. 9:7).

5. "Direct confrontation of sin is an American practice."

The person who said this has at least two wrong assumptions: (1) Americans make a habit of confronting each other with sin, and (2) if Americans do something, it is bad.

As to the first point, we wish American Christians actually did confront each other with their sin. Then perhaps American evangelical churches would not tolerate the sins of pride, rebellion, lust, impurity, idolatry, gossip, strife, and selfishness that permeate their pews, and often affect the overseas workers they send out. The fact is, we have found that Americans are particularly loathe to confront. Even if Americans did practice healthy confrontation as much as the Bible calls for, their rebuke of others would not be disqualified just because they were Americans. After all, let us not forget that we get our model for confrontation from Jesus, a Jewish Palestinian, and from Paul, a Jewish Asian.

Americans or Northern Europeans who do not want to appear as domineering or forceful on international teams or in MBB fellowships often hesitate to do peacemaking. While we commend sensitivity to cross-cultural dynamics, we also must encourage *any* peacemaker from *any* ethnic or national background to obey the commands of Scripture to gently, lovingly, compassionately, and firmly rebuke sin in whomever it is found.

6. "Encouraging someone to admit sin to other people is inappropriate in 'shame' cultures."

While accepting that the biblical principle of rebuking an offender's sin and expecting him to confess to others is appropriate in so-called Western or Judeo-Christian "guilt" cultures, many people observe that calling for verbal admission of sin violates deeply ingrained social norms in "shame" cultures. We agree with this observation, but disagree with those who then conclude that we should not do peacemaking in shame cultures the way the Bible teaches it.

Often even the most godly believers in shame cultures are reluctant to verbally admit their sins to other people. This is understandable from a cultural viewpoint, but not from a biblical one. There are few Bible commands as clear and simple as "confess your sins to one another" (James 5:16). The Greek word used in the verse, *exomologeo*, means "a public acknowledgement or confession of sins." Just as the commands, "forgive one another" or "do not commit adultery" or "do not steal" must be followed at the expense of accepted social norms in some cultures, the biblical practice of public confession of sin must be followed even in shame cultures.

Some peacemakers living in shame cultures have found creative ways to help MBBs confess their sins to others. For example, one patient peacemaker leads an unconfessed offender in prayer for the effects of his sin on himself and others. While in prayer, the peacemaker encourages the offender to confess his sin to Jesus. In this way, the offender who confesses his sin to Jesus while in prayer with a peacemaker effectively admits his sin to the peacemaker as well. We commend how this peacemaker goes the extra mile in helping shame culture members confess their sin. Of course, we must point out that the offender's repentance in prayer is not the end of the peacemaking process. His deeds of righteousness must still be openly demonstrated to any person he has sinned against.

7. "Doesn't your peacemaking go too far, too deep, too soon?"

A leader in a sending agency's home office noticed that the teams we lead and oversee tend to lose first-term members at a higher rate than other teams. This agency leader respectfully asked us if perhaps the reason for so much loss was that our peacemaking with new expat workers goes "too far, too deep, too soon." This is a good question, and has implications not just for peacemaking with new team members, but for discipling new MBBs as well.

Let us start with the issue of peacemaking with first-term expat team members. All of us know the stresses, strains, difficulties, and challenges of an inexperienced team member. He has to adjust to a new culture, new language, new food, new dress, new identity, new job, new ministry, new coworkers. These adjustments cause stress, and stress causes fatigue in body, mind, and spirit. Stress and fatigue create an environment for intense temptations that the TM may never have faced before. He may respond to these trials by criticizing locals and local culture, displaying outbursts of anger, sinking into depression, questioning and challenging team leadership, mistreating his wife and children, neglecting his responsibilities, or indulging his fleshly appetites. His actions and reactions may surprise himself ("I'm not really like this" or "I wasn't like this before"), which leads to even more stress. He may excuse himself and blame others for his suffering.

The sending agency leader questioned the wisdom of confronting sin in a person who is facing so much stress and change. The thought is, though we certainly can't close our eyes to sin, shouldn't we wait until the team member is through the first term's struggles before we work on character issues? Isn't it unloving and unfair to pressure him even more?

We appreciate this leader's concern for new team members, particularly ones whom he has recently recruited and oriented. *We are also concerned for new team members; we want them to be the best ambassadors for the Messiah that they can be.* That's why we believe it is imperative to do peacemaking with them from the start. In fact, the first term is a once-in-a-lifetime window of opportunity for growth. Dick Scoggins illustrates the concept of suffering and trials in a person's life as a dam holding back a lake of water. The dam of a person's life has cracks and weak spots in it, but as long as the weather is calm and the water behind the dam is smooth, the dam can hold back the lake. However, when wind rages and whips up waves that pound against the dam, the dam's cracks and weak spots become exposed. In this analogy, the stresses faced by a first termer are the wind and the waves which expose the cracks and weak spots in his character. Rather than coddle the sins of a new team member in the name of empathy for his stress, we should look at revelation of sin in the first term as a wonderful opportunity for his transformation.

Here it is absolutely imperative to remember that the stresses of a first term worker do not *create* character weaknesses in him; they merely *expose* pre-existing character faults. A steel bridge looks strong as it spans a river until heavy traffic exposes its cracks and it eventually buckles. First-term trials show a man exactly how strong — or weak — he really is, without the artificial support of a busy home church ministry and abundant fellowship. When the true self of the man is revealed, he is often shocked at how sinful he is. Some men are broken by the Spirit, thankful for the revelation, and repent in deep, godly sorrow (2 Cor. 7:10).

However, some men resist revelation, and we have to continue peacemaking, that is, the discipline and restoration process. Usually, if an offender continues to resist our peacemaking, he calls on his home church to advocate for him. Because they have never seen the man's true sinful self, his home church pastor and elders (a) cannot believe that their man has acted like we have observed, and (b) blame us for compounding the stress the man is under. In addition, since most churches do not believe in or practice peacemaking, they vilify us and our peacemaking with words like abusive, harsh, unhealthy, and in one case, hell.

If exposed sin is not repented of — in the first term or any other time in life — the offender's heart is likely to become calloused and that much less open to future revelation, to his peril (Prov. 29:1). He will probably devise ways to hide his sin again, until, as Scoggins says, "the devil decides to use it." No, our peacemaking in the first term is not "too soon."

Now, does our peacemaking go "too far, too deep?"

We practice peacemaking much like we do evangelism. In evangelism, we first listen to discern the mind and heart of the person we are talking with. We explain a bit of truth and we call for a step of response to that truth. If the man responds to the truth, we reveal more and more until he understands enough to repent and believe. If he refuses to respond to smaller bits of truth, we keep the relationship open, but we also gently warn him about the consequences of his resistance. However, we do not invest increasing amounts of time in those who do not respond to clear revelation.

In peacemaking among believers, we pray, we search our own hearts, we get the logs out of our own eyes, and then we listen with patience, compassion, and discernment to all parties involved. Then we reveal truth to the offender by correcting the most obvious, surface, or fruit sin (what Scoggins calls the presentation sin). If the offender responds with righteous acts after repenting from his fruit sin, he is often open to revelation of his root sin. We encourage him to go farther and farther, deeper and deeper into his heart to repent on the root level. Those who respond positively find joyous release and transformation into the image of Christ and are enthusiastically appreciative of our efforts.

Our sending agency leader friend has no problem with this scenario. His question comes when the team member or MBB refuses to repent on some level and yet we continue the peacemaking process. Or, in his words, we go "too far and too deep" when the offender cries, "Enough!"

If a believer refuses to respond to revelation at any point, we are obligated to treat him differently than we would an unregenerate person. We cannot just let him go his own way. We must urge him, implore him, on Christ's behalf to be reconciled to God (2 Cor. 5:20), and continue to bring revelation to him until he either repents and is restored or he forces us to go through the entire biblical discipline process. This is the imperative of biblical peacemaking.

Going far and deep in peacemaking is simply obedience to biblical commands. Love's manual lists the verses that teach us to rebuke each other. *In fact, if we do not go far and deep in our peacemaking, we sin ourselves.* Proverbs 24:11-12 warns us not to let a brother continue in sin, because God will hold us accountable: "Deliver those who are being taken away to death, and those who are staggering to slaughter, oh hold them back. If you say, 'See, we did not know this,' does He not consider it who weighs the hearts? And does He not know it who keeps your soul? And will He not render to man according to his work?" On a more fundamental level, the law of love demands that we do to others what we want them to do for us (Matt. 7:12). If we fall into unconfessed sin, deaf to the voice of our conscience, the Word, and the Holy Spirit, do we not hope that our brothers will show their love for us by shining light on our sin and showing us the way out of the darkness? Do we not want them to go as far and as deep as it takes to rescue us from slaughter? Of course we do.

Sending agency personnel and home church pastors and elders have questioned the depth we go to in bringing revelation into so-called personal areas of an offender, such as his marriage or his past, in which he may have been deeply hurt. Our role as peacemaker is challenged even more when an offender has had, or is in, counseling with a professional Christian psychologist and that psychologist is not committed to biblical peacemaking as taught by Love and Scoggins.

While we recognize that many North Americans are coming to the field from broken, dysfunctional homes and abusive childhoods, we have to ask some hard questions. When a cp team member's sin inhibits his effectiveness as an ambassador for the Messiah, are we supposed to ignore his sin if he has a past which prevents him from receiving loving, compassionate correction without having an emotional crisis? One coach of field workers told us that in a conference at which he spoke, 80% of the attendees raised their hands when he asked them if they had ever been "abused by authority." If a team member feels he has been abused by authority somewhere in his past, does this give him exemption from submitting to his present authority (Heb. 13:17)? We think not.

If our recruits are still so hurt by their past that they cannot receive or practice biblical peacemaking on the field, we should tell them, "Thank you very much for applying, but if you cannot or will not receive peacemaking done by field authority persons, then we cannot take you at this time, but would welcome you to come back when you are emotionally, psychologically, and spiritually able to do so."

8. "You should wait to rebuke until the offender is ready to hear your correction."

We agree that timing is certainly an important factor in peacemaking. The peacemaker needs to have discernment regarding the appropriate moment and venue to initiate the process. However, the above claim springs from two faulty assumptions: (1) the offender has the right to determine when he receives rebuke ("I'm not ready to talk about this yet"); (2) the offender has the right to determine who brings rebuke to him ("I'm not ready to hear this *from* you"). Notice that the offender claims the right to determine both the *who* and the *when* of the peacemaking process. This self-centeredness by the offender is the opposite of humility and contrary to biblical peacemaking.

We have found that when an offender says, "I am not ready" he is almost always really saying, "I am *not willing.*" In effect, he is saying, "*I* will control when I discuss this issue and I will control with whom I discuss it." By making this claim, he is also reserving the right to perpetually refuse correction in general, and/or to perpetually refuse correction from the offended or any peacemaker who is not of his liking. This claim only strengthens the selfishness (note the prolific use of "I") that probably caused him to be an offender in the first place, and must be corrected if he is to repent and be reconciled to God and man.

Nowhere in Scripture do we see any hint of the idea that an offender has the option of choosing either his accuser or the timing of his correction. Matthew 18:15 does not say, "If the brother who has sinned is ready to hear you, then go and show him his sin." It simply says, "If your brother sins, go." Neither does that verse say, "Make sure that the brother who has sinned approves of you as a peacemaker before you go to him."

"Earn the right to be heard" is a popular principle in modern ministry mentality. We understand that its original intent was to enlighten teachers, disciplers, and evangelists to the idea that if they gain the respect and trust of the persons they want to influence, their message will receive a better hearing and thus be more effective. This has merit in many contexts, and we always try to win the trust of an offender by listening with care, warmth, and empathy. However, while it is convenient and desirable if a peacemaker has somehow been able to "earn the right to be heard" by the offender, it is by no means a biblical requirement in a discipline case. When a man sins, he does not gain the right to determine his accuser — it is just the opposite. A. W. Tozer counsels that we should be "ready to hear" from anyone: "When reproved pay no attention to the source. Do not ask whether it is a friend or an enemy that reproves you. An enemy is often of greater value to you than a friend because he is not influenced by sympathy." (*The Root of the Righteous*)

9. "Where is grace in your peacemaking?"

We often hear this from those whom we've confronted with their sin, but who have not listened or repented. They feel pressure and are irritated because we keep the light on their sin. They lash out and accuse us of not showing them grace. They want us to terminate the peacemaking process so they can scurry back comfortably into the darkness of their sin. Their feeling is that if we were loving, we would show them this kind of grace. After all, doesn't God, who is love, show grace?

The irony — and tragedy — of this situation is that while the offender claims to be seeking grace, he doesn't recognize that grace is exactly what we are offering. We listen with with gentleness and empathy, *and* we counsel him with the Word of God: "God gives grace..." But unlike the practice of some, we also quote the whole context in which these words are found: "*God is opposed to the proud*, but gives grace *to the humble*" (1 Pet. 5:5, Jas. 4:6, cf. Prov. 3:34). We beg him to turn from his self-protecting, self-serving, and ultimately self-defeating pride. We urge him, we implore him, on Christ's behalf, to be reconciled to God by humbling himself under God's mighty hand, so that God will lift him up at the proper time (1 Pet. 5:6).

No man in history who has confessed his pride and humbled himself before God has failed to find grace. True grace is found in repentance, not in resistance.

10. "We're not opposed to peacemaking, we're opposed to the way you do it."

Two fallacies lurk behind this challenge: (1) a peacemaker's real or perceived mistakes in method invalidate the process; (2) the peacemaker and his method must be approved by the offender before peacemaking can take place.

We'll be the first to admit that we are not perfect and we need to constantly upgrade our peacemaking skills. But that said, behind the above statement lies a belief that we've often encountered: if the peacemaker violates a spoken or unspoken protocol (according to the offender or his advocate) during the discipline process, the offender feels he is released from any responsibility for that particular sin. The situation is like a criminal case which is thrown out of court on a technicality; the arresting officer didn't read the suspect his rights, or the prosecution violated rules in gathering evidence. It is sad enough that the guilty go free on a technicality in the world outside the Kingdom, but when such appeals are made in biblical peacemaking, it is simply tragic.

Quite often, peacemakers who are not confident of their skill wait too long to confront an offender who has an unapproachable, blustery spirit and they end up admonishing the offender in haste or anger. This can degenerate into an examination of the peacemaker rather than the offender, and if the offender is particularly articulate and of a strong will, he can derail the whole process. But when an offender claims he is exempt from discipline because a peacemaker has been clumsy, insensitive or ill-timed in his rebuke, this says more about the offender than the peacemaker. It says that the offender is not teachable, humble, or open to admonition. The Bible uses a stronger word: "he who hates reproof is stupid" (Prov 12:1).

A wise, mature believer will not just be open to rebuke from those he chooses or trusts or likes. He will not reject correction because the peacemaker is an authority, a peer, a man, a woman, married, single, a first termer, a veteran, a local or an expat. He will seek it from wherever and whomever he can find it, and be thankful for the Great Shepherd's comforting rod and staff of discipline.

11. "We do not have to rebuke sin in mature believers; we can trust God to speak to them in His time."

Of course God does bring revelation of sin to an individual without other people's intervention. Men's consciences (Rom. 2:14-15), the Scriptures (2 Tim. 3:16-17, Heb. 4:12-13), and the Holy Spirit (John 16:8) can each convict a person of sin. We believe every gathering of the church for worship should have a time for meditation on Matt. 5:23-24 so that every person can have the opportunity to "remember" that his brother or sister has something against him and be reconciled before continuing worship. How happy is the man who is so sensitive to God's voice that he receives revelation from one or more of these means and repents on his own. *However, the truth is that not every believer — not even a "mature" one — always hears the convicting voice of God on his own.* And hearing God's voice isn't the only problem. Some, having heard the Spirit speak through his conscience or the Word, choose to ignore Him.

King David, the man after God's own heart, was so dull to his sin with Bathsheba that the Lord had to send the prophet Nathan to rebuke him (2 Sam. 12:1). The Apostle Paul had to sharply admonish the Apostle Peter for his hypocrisy "to his face" in the assembly of church leaders (Gal. 2:11-14). Imagine what other sins David might have committed, further shaming the name of God, if Nathan had just hoped and prayed, but not rebuked him. And think of the huge implications for the expansion of the Kingdom among the Gentiles if Paul had not confronted Peter. If mature believers like David and Peter needed rebuke from the brethren, how much more do we? Knowing that we all need correction from people at some time, the Lord made sure the Bible contained ample teaching on peacemaking.

In the midst of a very difficult peacemaking situation, an uninformed sending agency leader said to us, "I trust Frank and Elizabeth to discern if there is sin in their marriage. They can hear God's voice, and if they say their marriage is OK, it's not your or my place to interfere." Non-biblical thinking like that behind this well-meaning but naive brother's statement often significantly hinders and lengthens the peacemaking process. We must realize that no one, even a mature believer, who becomes comfortable walking in unrepented sin is likely to receive revelation on his own. Wishful thinking and "giving the benefit of the doubt" are not acceptable substitutes for loving and obedient admonition from the brethren.

12. "You should not judge motives."

The term "judging motives" is one of the red penalty cards which modern Christians raise to stop peacemaking and block any further "pry-ing" into an offender's "personal life." (Of course, the offended never realize that when they pull out their "Do not judge motives" red card, they are in fact judging our motives!) We will not cover the subject of judging other believers here (though we recommend a careful reading of 1 Cor. 5:12-6:11). We acknowledge that it is possible to judge others' motives in an ungodly manner, and that this can be ruinous to peacemaking. A good peacemaker knows this, and will constantly monitor his own motives during the peacemaking process. We will now discuss how to reveal and discern motives in a godly way during peacemaking.

True peace and transformation come when we repent of sin on the deepest level. Dick Scoggins calls our most basic beliefs and values Affections. From these roots sprout our Attitudes, or branches, which then lead to our Actions, or fruit. The peacemaking process involves tracing fruit sin down through its branches to its roots. Another way to say this is that we go from the What (the presentation sin of word or action) to the Why (the attitude and affection) which caused the fruit sin. Repentant offenders are overcome with joy when we help them see the wrong thoughts and beliefs about God, themselves and other people from which their sins have sprouted. They experience release from the bondage of unbiblical thinking and ungodly beliefs and are eager to renew their minds (Rom. 12:2). When an offender understands and repents of a root sin, many fruit sins besides the presentation sin dry up and fall away. The offender is radically transformed into a new stage of glory.

We admit that when we search for the reasons an offender has sinned, we are indeed investigating his motives, that is, what motivates him to sin. (Whistle! Intentional foul! Red card! Booo!)

The reason we are not ashamed to search out motives in an offender is that God Himself is ultimately more concerned about *why* we do what we do than He is about *what* we do. Look at Matt. 6:1-18 and the Lord's warnings about right motivation in praying, fasting, and giving money to religion. He discerned and rebuked the Pharisees' evil motives when they asked him trick questions. He saw that Judas' kiss in Gethsemane was anything but a greeting of affection from a trusted friend. He challenged the disciples, "*Why* do you fear? *Why* do you not see the log in your own eye? *Why* are you anxious? *Why* do you not believe?" Jesus traced fruit to roots. He was after the *why* behind the *what*. He questioned motives.

Offenders who do not want their motives exposed before men here on earth are in for a rude awakening. "And there is no creature hidden from His sight, but all things are open and laid bare to the eyes of Him with whom we have to do" (Heb. 4:13). "God will judge the secrets of men through Christ Jesus" (Rom. 2:16). He "will both bring to light the things hidden in the darkness and disclose the motives of men's hearts" (1 Cor 4:5).

Rather than vainly attempting to hide our motives from His eternal spotlight, how much better it is for us to pray with the Psalmist, "Search me, try me, know me, and see if there is any hurtful way in me" (Ps. 139:23-24). Why would a believer who has entrusted himself to his Father who judges all men impartially (1 Pet. 1:17) not entrust himself to loving peacemakers who rightly handle the Word of truth which is "able to judge the thoughts and intentions of the heart" (Heb. 4:12)? Is it not in our best interest to have our motives revealed to us by the Word and the brethren and repent of them here rather than wait until we are face-to-face with the Master? On that day when He finally judges our motives, we will not have the option to blow a whistle, cry foul, and flash a red card in His face.

13. "Your peacemaking causes hurt feelings."

The attitude behind this thinly veiled condemnation is, "Spiritual encounters with God are always soft, warm, safe, comforting, and uplifting." So, when our peacemaking reveals the hard, cold, dangerous, threatening, and depressing causes and results of the sin of an offender who believes this, he naturally reacts strongly.

What could cause hurt feelings in an offender? Our experience shows that offenders can feel that they have been hurt by either one, or both, of two persons during peacemaking. The first is the human peacemaker. When an offender feels he has been hurt by a peacemaker, two possibilities arise. It is possible that the peacemaker may actually have sinned against the offender by not being biblically loving, compassionate, gentle, kind, or patient in the process. In this case, the offender must confront the peacemaker (who has become an offender!). The peacemaker must repent, and the offender must forgive him. But do not think that the peacemaker's sin in the process of peacemaking exonerates the offender from the sin he committed which caused the need for peacemaking in the first place.

On the other hand, while the offender may feel that the peacemaker has violated his biblical rights, it is possible that the offender is wrong in this assessment. He, in fact, may be sinning by taking offence at the godly efforts of the peacemaker. *A person's feelings are always **real**, but they are not always **right**.* For example, an offender may feel that a peacemaker is angry, harsh, or without grace in his treatment of the offender, but in reality the peacemaker may simply be speaking the truth in love. In these cases, it is the cold truth of the *message* that hurts the offender, not the *messenger*. We have had to say some hard things to those with whom we work:

>"You lied."
>"You deceived your leader."
>"You chose to disobey the Word of God."
>"You committed adultery in your heart."
>"You gossiped against your team leader."

"You do not believe God will provide for you."
"You broke your marriage covenant."
"You slandered your teammate."
"You love masturbation more than you love your wife or God."
"You despise your team member."
"You are arrogant."
"You are lazy."

Some of the offenders were "hurt" and "offended" by these statements. The words were "hard" and "cutting." We ought not be surprised by these reactions, for each of the above statements is based on or taken exactly from the Word of God, which is "sharper than any two-edged sword, and piercing as far as the division of soul and spirit" (Heb. 4:12). No matter how gently a peacemaker applies the scalpel of the Word, its piercing and cutting will "hurt" a sinful soul.

The apostle Paul, who penned the "love passage" in 1 Cor. 13, also made the Corinthians "sorry" with other parts of that letter. Here is how Paul responded to their hurt: "For though I caused you sorrow by my letter, I do not regret it; though I did regret it — for I see that that letter caused you sorrow, though only for a while — I now rejoice, not that you were made sorrowful, but that you were made sorrowful to the point of repentance; for you were made sorrowful according to the will of God, so that you might not suffer loss in anything through us. For the sorrow that is according to the will of God produces a repentance without regret, leading to salvation, but the sorrow of the world produces death" (2 Cor. 7:8-10).

Paul, the model peacemaker, hurt the offenders he confronted. This caused him both regret and joy. He regretted hurting them, like a caring father wishes he didn't have to discipline his children. But he could rejoice because the sorrow he caused them was according to the will of God and they responded with repentance.

God is the second person who can "hurt" an offender during peacemaking. The believer who thinks that his Heavenly Father is only gentle and safe does not know Him well enough. While our Heavenly Father loves us and provides for our every need, He also disciplines those sons whom He loves (Heb. 12:5-11). His discipline may not make us happy, and may temporarily hurt. "All discipline for the moment seems not to be joyful, but sorrowful; yet to those who have been trained by it, afterwards it yields the peaceful fruit of righteousness" (Heb. 12:11).

Offenders who wish the God of love to be "gentle" and "safe" during the peacemaking process need to listen to Mr. Beaver from C. S. Lewis' *The Lion, the Witch and the Wardrobe*. When the human children first heard about Aslan the lion from Mr. & Mrs. Beaver, they asked, "But is he quite safe?" Mr. Beaver replied, "Safe? Who said anything about safe? 'Course he isn't safe. But he is *good*. He's the King, I tell you" [italics added]. The Good King, our Heavenly Father loves us even when His discipline hurts us. So our good and loving peacemaking in His name will also "hurt" offenders.

14. "You should not exhort anyone to be confronted by a peacemaker whom he fears."

Fear, with one notable exception, always negatively affects peacemaking.

A peacemaker may be afraid that if he confronts sin in a coworker or MBB, he will break the relationship. His fear turns him into a peace*keeper* who neglects his loving duty to his brother. The irony of not rebuking sin for fear of breaking a relationship is that the very reason the peacemaker needs to confront a brother is precisely because a relationship is already broken. The offender has broken his relationship with God, and probably with other people.

Perhaps a peacemaker is afraid of his own sin being exposed and/or his reputation being tarnished. If so, he should trust God to glorify Himself in the peacemaking process and realize that if indeed his own sin is exposed, that this is a win-win opportunity for him. He simply needs to repent, receive grace and forgiveness. Then he is free to bring these gifts to the offender.

The same is true of an offender. He may refuse revelation because he thinks that if he admits his guilt, his reputation will be stained. This is fear of man rather than of God, which is probably a deeper sin than whatever he is being rebuked for. A man fearful of repentance does not trust in the One who offers the pearl of forgiveness and cleansing, which is worth much more than the price of his reputation and the righteousness that needs to follow repentance.

We have seen multiple cases when an offender refused to meet with the appropriate peacemaker, citing his "fear" of the peacemaker himself. The offender claimed the peacemaker was "intimidating," the implication being that the offender would be psychologically or emotionally wounded if this peacemaker were allowed to be in the process. The offender hoped that this appeal to emotion would somehow disqualify the peacemaker from confronting him. What the offender really meant by the peacemaker being intimidating was that the peacemaker was articulate, coolheaded, discerning, and skilled at identifying the offender's attitudes, words, and actions as biblical sin. Of course a peacemaker like this would be "intimidating" to an offender hoping to hide from the light! Note that this is just one of many "mirrors" used by offenders who hope to deflect the light off of themselves and back onto the peacemaker. Such offenders want us to think that the peacemaker is somehow at fault or in sin because he is wise, experienced, and knows how to rightly divide the Word of truth.

However, one type of fear is right. The offender, the offended, and the peacemaker should all share a common fear of the One with Whom they have to do, for "it is terrifying to fall into the hands of the living God" (Heb. 10:31).

15. "Shouldn't you make use of psychological concepts while peacemaking?"

We are not opposed to the use of appropriate psychological principles in peacemaking, any more than we are against the use of appropriate psychological principles in evangelism, personal discipleship, and body life in cp. The key word, of course, is appropriate. For a psychological concept to be appropriate, it must certainly not conflict with any biblical teaching, and it must enhance our understanding of biblical concepts. Given these criteria, we are free to use psychological terms and ideas in peacemaking.

However, since all Christians involved in peacemaking will know and believe the Bible, but not all will know and understand psychological concepts and terms, it is highly desirable that the vocabulary used in peacemaking be from the Bible and not from psychology. This has many advantages.

- Bible words have inherent spiritual power; psychological terms do not (Is. 55:11, Heb. 4:12, 2 Tim. 3:15-16).

- An offender will receive spiritual revelation much more quickly and clearly if his offense is explained to him using biblical words. It is the loving duty of the offended and the peacemaker to provide the offender with biblical terms so he can respond to the Bible rather than just the offended's expression of emotion or psychological state. Given that the goal of peacemaking is biblical reconciliation of the offender with the offended, then the offender needs to clearly comprehend and articulate the biblical sin which he committed so he can confess, repent, and be biblically forgiven by the offended. A man can no more repent of a word or action that is not a biblical sin than he can repent of having brown hair or blue eyes.

- The discipline of learning to use biblical vocabulary in peacemaking keeps our focus on the unchanging Word of God and constantly renews our faith in its transforming power (2 Tim. 3:15-16).

- Filling our minds and conversations with Bible words protects us from being wooed into using contemporary jargon or psychological terms in their place. Some Christian workers use psychological terms for relationship problems as if they are synonymous with the Bible's words for sin. At first glance, this seems harmless. You could even call it contextualisation for this generation. But you need to know that this can be dangerous and carries the potential for grave consequences. Once you believe that a psychological term means the same thing as a biblical word, then you have prepared your mind and conscience to use them interchangeably. Now, if your mind allows you to freely substitute a psychological term for the biblical word, then you *just might* accept psychological "treatment" for a man's "condition" as a substitute for biblical repentance for a man's sin.

Joseph, the child of overseas Christian workers, and his wife were from a famous megachurch. We had actively recruited them and had rejoiced that they had chosen our team over two other agencies. A couple of weeks after arriving on the field, Joseph came to share with us that he had been seeing a Christian counselor prior to leaving his home country. He told us that the Christian counselor had diagnosed him as having a "disease" called "addiction to lust." This disease caused Joseph to "act out" by viewing pornographic material, fantasising about having sex with women other than his wife, and masturbating. The Christian counselor taught Joseph that he would "always" have this disease, in the same way that an alcoholic will always be an alcoholic, and that Joseph's goal in life should be to remain "sober." Joseph requested that we regularly ask him if he was remaining sober.

At first, we saw the situation as positive, for three reasons:

(1) Joseph had come to us voluntarily with this information.

(2) Both Joseph and the Christian counselor saw that it was not good for Joseph to "act out" his sexual fantasies by masturbating.

(3) Joseph asked us to hold him accountable.

We accepted the Christian counselor's words as valid terms to describe Joseph's "condition." We accepted the Christian counselor's "treatment" as valid also.

However, it was only a few months until Joseph's bad fruit became intolerable. In regular accountability times, we saw that Joseph was not spending the required time in language learning nor reporting his language hours as we had instructed him to. He was not obeying the biblical commands for husbands. In ways small and large, he questioned and challenged our authority. He was also not remaining "sober." As we began peacemaking with Joseph, we used biblical terms for Joseph's situation. Instead of "acting out", we named his fantasising and masturbating as "adultery in his heart" (Matt. 5:28) and "impurity" (Gal. 5:19, Eph. 5:3, Col. 3:5). We described his "addiction to lust" not as a "disease" but as his choosing to let his lust entice him and carry him away into sin and death (Jas. 1:14-15). We showed that his seemingly noble goal of simply staying "sober" was actually self-centeredness ("*I* am struggling with *my* disease,"

"Pray that I remain sober today") and not proactive love focused on others (Matt. 7:12) or considering others more important than himself (Phil. 2:3). Joseph verbally repented of these sins, but over time he did not bring forth fruits in keeping with repentance (Matt. 3:8).

During months of peacemaking, we asked questions that revealed his deepest root sin. When we asked him if he believed God wanted him to be transformed and totally free from his sin, Joseph insisted on continuing to call his struggles a disease. We explained 1 Cor. 6:9-11 and pointed out that if he was regenerate, then he had a new nature and he was no longer an adulterer, a fornicator, or even a "drunkard" because "Such were some of you; but you were washed, but you were sanctified, but you were justified in the name of the Lord Jesus Christ and in the Spirit of our God" (v. 11). We asked Joseph if he believed God had given him a new nature and could change his flesh. His answer was, "No." He said that his sickness was something God created him with, and therefore wanted him to live with. We eventually had to discipline Joseph off the team and off the field for his refusal to repent of the root sin from which all his other sins came from — the sin of unbelief in God and his Word.

You can see how labeling his sin with psychological terms helped keep Joseph in darkness. By calling his sin a "disease," he chose to believe that it was like a congenital physical illness such as diabetes or cystic fibrosis. Therefore, Joseph did not believe he was a new creature in Christ, nor that he was spiritually responsible for his continued practice of sin. By preferring psychological terms over the authority of Scripture, Joseph demonstrated that the root sin under his impurity, the adultery in his heart, his disobedience to the commands for husbands, his rebellion against authority (including God's) was his self-centeredness, pride and arrogance. Joseph would not listen to us or to God Himself. Because he would not listen and did not believe God, we put Joseph out of our fellowship, treated him as an unbeliever (Matt. 18:17) and warned his home church to do the same.

Sadly, Joseph was welcomed back in his home church, apparently without question. Joseph wrote a newsletter to his supporters saying that the reason he left the field was that our field personnel "did not have the resources to deal with his problems."

> [As a partially positive postscript, we heard from a third party that Joseph gave a public testimony in a church seven years after leaving the field in which he confessed that he had been rightly disciplined off our team. We would rejoice to hear this confession from Joseph personally, as evidence of his complete repentance.]

Ironically, Christian psychologists who use biblical words to reveal sin to an unrepentant client provoke the same reactions we non-psychologists do. At their sending agency's recommendation, Charles and Mary received weeks of pre-field marriage counseling from a professional. This continued by email on the field, and with the full knowledge of the TL and wife. For over a year, the TL and wife held Charles and Mary accountable to their counselor's biblical advice. When certain sins were revealed, Charles and Mary began to reject the light. The TL and wife patiently kept bringing revelation to Charles and Mary because they judged that Charles and Mary's marriage-related sins were keeping them from fruitful ministry. The professional Christian counselor agreed with the TL and wife. Eventually, Charles and Mary unilaterally announced their resignation from the team, terminated their relationship with the counselor, and demanded that the counselor speak no more to their sending agency's personnel about them (a legally-binding action).

Meanwhile, Charles and Mary found several advocates at home. One recommended that the TL not use the word "sin" in a peacemaking meeting because it was a "strong" word. These advocates overruled the TL's and Christian counselor's biblically worded evaluations of sin in Charles and Mary's marriage and refused to listen to their warnings of the dangers associated with that sin. Instead, using popular non-biblical measures and vocabulary, the advocates determined that Charles and Mary's marriage was "not in trouble" and that they were fit for overseas service.

Again, remember that most MBBs (and many TLs and TMs) have no access to contemporary psychological terms and concepts, but they do have access to the Bible. *The less we rely on psychological terms and the more we depend on Bible words in our peacemaking, our ministry is that much more reproducable.* Besides, our dependence upon biblical vocabulary and skill at using the Bible as our peacemaking manual communicates to MBBs that our authority is the unchanging Word, and not Western thought. The time and effort we could spend on teaching MBBs psychological concepts is better invested in teaching them the vocabulary of biblical peacemaking.

16. "You try to trap people with their own words."

As Love's manual emphasises, it is impossible to understate the importance of careful listening and speaking in peacemaking. Sometimes peacemaking is happily and quickly completed when the offended and offender come face-to-face and discover that the cause of their conflict was merely a misunderstanding of words. But normally peacemaking involves much listening and sorting through words to find the causes of the sin and broken relationship.

A skilled peacemaker will be very careful to note the exact words that the offended and offender use during the peacemaking process. He does this to separate emotions and feelings from facts and to assist both the offended and the offender to articulate the offence in question as a biblical sin. Rather than "trap" the offender, sometimes our efforts at careful listening to words actually show that the offended cannot make a biblical case for his complaint. Then the roles become reversed; the original offended must repent of bringing a false accusation against the original offender.

We admit that many resistant offenders *feel* like we are trying to trap them with their own words. Several have said to us, "I feel like I have to be careful with every word I say around you. I'm afraid that whatever I say, you will use it against me." In our experience, these kinds of statements reveal three things.

(a) The offender does not trust our motives in the peacemaking process.

To which we ask, Why would we want to "trap" him? Does he think that we do not have better things to do with our time than to interrogate an innocent person until he nervously blurts something that is not true? On the contrary, we are trying to win him (Matt 18:15), to restore him (Gal. 6:1) and to reconcile him to God and man so he can be an exemplary ambassador for Christ. In fact, we are trying to free him from the trap of his own sin.

(b) The offender has something to hide from us and God.

In that case, he is right to be afraid, "For the mouth speaks out of that which fills the heart" (Matt. 12:34). If his heart is full of evil treasure, he will not be able to stop it from eventually popping out of his mouth. But if the offender's heart overflows with good treasure, his words will prove it, and he should have no fear of us or God. Our peacemaking simply speeds up the flow.

(c) The offender feels like he does not have to be careful what he says around other people.

We remind the offender and ourselves of our Lord's promise: "But I tell you that every careless word that people speak, they shall give an accounting for it in the day of judgment. For by your words you will be justified, and by your words you will be condemned" (Matt. 12:36-37).

While we were in the information gathering phase of peacemaking, we patiently listened to a team member, Tom. He gave lengthy and disjointed discourses in response to our questions. Without accusation, we commented that he takes a long time to get his point across.

Tom replied, "Yeah, I just kind of throw things out there and let people catch what they can. I'm not real organized when I talk. But what I really want to say is in there somewhere."

We said, "For example, in a paragraph of ten disjointed sentences, what you really want to say is sentence number nine, and you hope your listener hangs in there until he gets it."

Tom chuckled. "Yeah, that's right. That's a good way to put it."

We then pointed out that Tom's sloppiness in speech was not loving to his listener. By not disciplining himself to think through what he is going to say, Tom places the burden of communication on the listener, who has to sort through volumes of words and then guess what Tom really means. Tom's speech pattern also allows him to conveniently disclaim anything he says which he is called to account for:

> We: "Tom, during your monologue a few minutes ago we heard you say,..."
>
> Tom: "No, I didn't mean that. What I meant was (ten more sentences)."

Torrential talkers like Tom get very uncomfortable when careful listeners do peacemaking with them. But resistant offenders who are guarded and frugal with their words also dislike a peacemaker's careful listening and accurate memory. Their fewer words are easier for the peacemaker to keep track of!

Christ's ambassadors, of all people, must be careful and persuasive communicators, whether they are naturally talkative or naturally quiet. If the peacemaking process reveals that a man cannot articulate his ideas clearly, that he is afraid of what he will say if someone listens carefully, or that he resists being held accountable for his words, this may be a sign that he ought not to be on the field at all.

17. "Your peacemaking is too authoritarian."

Never forget that the need for peacemaking only arises because the offender has rebelled against authority. By that we mean that he has sinned. John Piper reminds us that all sin is an act of rebellion against the King's decrees, or an exchange of our own glory for that which is rightfully God's:

> "All sin comes from not putting supreme value on the glory of God. And we all have sinned. 'None is righteous, no not one' (Romans 3:10). None of us has trusted God the way we should. None of us has obeyed him according to his wisdom and right. We have exchanged and dishonored his glory again and again. We have trusted ourselves. We have taken credit for his gifts. We have turned away from the path of his commandments because we thought we knew better." (*Desiring God* p. 56-57)

When an offender resists peacemaking, he is simply continuing in his attitude of rebellion in which he committed his initial sin. In Piper's words, the offender thinks he knows better than God and the peacemaker. The offender resisted God's authority when he sinned, so we should not be surprised if he resists the peacemaker's and the church's God-given authority to bring him to repentance. Matthew 18:15-17 describes this as the offender's "not listening" to peacemakers.

Offenders and their advocates from many cultures cite numerous historical examples of the misuse of authority as excuses for them to resist the authority of the peacemaker. Northern Europeans remind us of Hitler's reign of terror. Latins, Asians, and Africans list the excesses of various colonial powers. Americans testify to abuse at the hands of church authorities during their youth. Those who know any sending agency's history can also point to instances when higher authority has allowed field team leaders to sin and lord it over team members, causing personal hurt and the disintegration of teams. These examples, combined with the postmodern generation's general suspicion of authority and value of relativism, give a resistant offender what he thinks is ample reason to judge the peacemaker's authority as invalid. The words authority and submission have almost become taboos.

The problem is, we cannot change the Bible's teachings on peacemaking in some misguided effort to make reparations for historical abuses or to allay the fears of an offender that the peacemaker might abuse his position of leadership. Every step of peacemaking calls for the offender to submit to the peacemaker's God-given spiritual authority, and the ultimate disciplinary step of excommunication is taken because the offender "does not listen" to the authority of the church.

Some peacemakers balk at taking authority because they have logs in their own eyes or their lives are otherwise not a good example. The win-win solution for this, of course, is for the peacemaker to repent. When he can say to the offender, "Do as I do" (Phil 4:9), he appeals to a type of authority that is not even dependent upon his position or office. This is one of the beautiful benefits of practicing peacemaking; everyone involved has a chance to be transformed. On the other hand, both the peacemaker and the offender lose if the peacemaker shrinks back from using his authority. Both end up in sin.

Resistant offenders can rebel against the peacemaker's authority in many ways. Here are just a few examples we have seen on field cp teams. We have observed similar patterns in MBB churches and fellowships.

(a.) *He claims he is accountable to a different authority than the peacemaker.*

A resistant offender will typically appeal to his home pastor, a coach, or someone else in his agency who he thinks will become his advocate because he "wasn't heard or understood" by the peacemaker. (We have found that when an offender claims he wasn't "heard," the truth is usually that the peacemaker indeed did *listen* to the offender. The peacemaker simply did not *agree* with him.) When the offender finds someone willing to advocate for him, the offender will then claim he has the right to recognize only the advocate's authority in his life. This, of course, violates the authority structure the offender placed himself under when he signed up with the agency.

Similarly, an MBB resistant offender will typically deny the authority of a peacemaker and claim to recognize only the authority of an elder or foreign worker who advocates for him.

(b.) Recognizing that the peacemaker has authority over him, the resistant offender tries to escape from peacemaking by officially taking himself out from under that authority.

Typically, resistant offenders will resign from their team or their church unilaterally (usually citing "personality" or "theological" differences). Or, a home church advocate will encourage the offender to leave the team in an effort to escape the light the peacemaker is bringing. In both cases, the offender feels a temporary (and false) relief from the godly pressure of the Word. But this is short-sighted on two points:

(1) If the offender wants to stay within his agency, the peacemaking must come to a positive biblical conclusion before he can join another team within that agency. He will still have to face the peacemaker and the original authority structure.

(2) If the offender resigns from his agency (or an MBB leaves his church or fellowship) completely, he loses an opportunity for transformation that he will probably not receive from his advocates. Rarely do home churches continue the peacemaking process, especially in the case of a sending church pulling its offending member off of a field team because the home church disagreed with our peacemaking. It is extremely doubtful that any group which receives an MBB escaping the peacemaking of another fellowship will do peacemaking with him.

(c.) The offender claims ignorance of the agency's authority structure, as if his so-called ignorance invalidates that authority.

This is expressed in many ways: "Who said my field leader could pry into my personal life?" "I was never told about the accountability or recourse policy." "The field manual doesn't say that the TL can tell me what to do."

We observe that offenders who are humble and teachable during peacemaking do not question authority, let alone rebel against it. Jesus commended a Roman centurion for his respect for authority, exclaiming that He had not seen such faith in Israel (Luke 7:2-10). As we practice peacemaking, we, too, must respect the authority God has both placed us under and given to us.

CONCLUSION

"Blessed are the peacemakers, for they shall be called sons of God" (Matt. 5:9). If you have not done much peacemaking, or have tried and failed, after reading these notes you probably wonder where the "blessed" part comes in. As we said in the introduction, we are both committed to and enthusiastic about peacemaking, even though it is costly. We are committed to it because it is commanded by Christ Himself; we are enthusiastic about it because we have seen it "work" in us, in our teammates, and in our MBB disciples. We think that obeying Christ and seeing the good fruit of renewal in our own and others' lives is worth the heavy investment.

As you have read above, peacemaking is difficult with people who resist admitting they have sinned even in the face of clear evidence, and who want to preserve their pride. Some agencies' and MBB fellowships' most visible and publicised ministry "producers" have disqualified themselves from the race by their own arrogance, despite Herculean efforts by peacemakers. Nevertheless, we persevere in begging and persuading men to be reconciled to God because we know what it means to fear God and we are controlled by the love of Christ (2 Cor. 5:11-20). But let us warn you: if you do not know the fear of God and if you are not compelled by Christ's love, you will surely become discouraged in peacemaking.

Thankfully, there is good news. Some brothers and sisters, after the patient, faithful efforts of peacemakers, eventually respond in humility, brokenness (in the biblical sense), and contrition. They open their lives to their good Father's loving discipline and they receive the full measure of His grace. They gain victory over strongholds of sin, they reconcile with all men and women, they cleanse their consciences, and they bear fruit that remains and multiplies. Seeing God entrust these humble ones with precious MBB relationships is worth all of the courage, patience, prayer, emails, money, travel, telephone calls, and late-night meetings that it took for them to finally admit to God and His peacemakers, "I've been blind and hard of heart; what you've shown me is true. I've sinned, and now I repent."

Do not shrink back from peacemaking because it is difficult and costly. In the fear of God and under the control of Christ's love, make whatever investment or sacrifice it takes. Your peacemaking is a love offering to God, and is *essential* for the health of both teams and churches.

Bibliography

Adams, Jay E.
- 1973 *The Christian Counselor's Manual*
  Grand Rapids: Baker Book House
- 1979 *A Theology of Christian Counseling*
  Grand Rapids: Zondervan Publishing House
- 1981 "Church Discipline," in *Update on Christian Counseling*
  Volumes 1 and 2, 69-74
  Grand Rapids: Zondervan Publishing House
- 1986 *Handbook of Church Discipline*
  Grand Rapids: Zondervan Publishing House

Adamson, James
- 1976 *The Epistle of James*
  Grand Rapids: Eerdmans Publishing Co.

Augsburger, David W.
- 1992 *Conflict Mediation Across Cultures*
  Louisville: Westminster/John Knox Press

Berkouwer, G.C.
- 1976 *The Church*
  Grand Rapids: Eerdmans Publishing Co.

Carson, D.A.
- 1984 "Matthew," in *The Expositor's Bible Commentary*
  Frank E. Gaebelein, General Editor
  Grand Rapids: Zondervan Publishing House

Davids, Peter H.
    1989   *James*
            Peabody: Hendrickson Publishers

De Koster, L.
    1990   "Church Discipline," in
            Evangelical Dictionary of Theology, 238
            Grand Rapids: Baker Book House

Elmer, Duane
    1993   *Cross-Cultural Conflict:*
            Building Relationships for Effective Ministry
            Downers Grove: InterVarsity PressFee, Gordon

Fee, Gordon
    1988   *1 and 2 Timothy, Titus*
            New International Biblical Commentary
            Peabody: Hendrickson Publishers

Fenton, Horace, L.
    1987   *When Christians Clash*
            Downers Grove: InterVarsity Press

Frame, John M.
    1991   *Evangelical Reunion*
            Grand Rapids: Baker Book House.

France, R. T.
    1985   *Matthew* Leicester: InterVarsity Press
            Grand Rapids: Eerdmans Publishing Co.

Grudem, Wayne
    1994   *Systematic Theology*
            Grand Rapids: Zondervan Publishing House

Gundry, Robert H.
    1982   *Matthew*
            Grand Rapids: Eerdmans Publishing Co.

Habermas, Ronald &
Issler, Klaus
    1992   *Teaching for Reconciliation*
            Grand Rapids: Baker Book House

Hesselgrave, David J.
    1984   *Counseling Cross Culturally*
            Grand Rapids: Baker Book House

Hession, Roy
    1977   *The Calvary Road*
              Fort Washington: Christian Literature Crusade

Kelly, J. N. D.
    1986   *A Commentary on the Pastoral Epistle*
              Grand Rapids: Baker Book House

Kirby, G.W.
    1977   "The Church," in *The Zondervan Pictorial Encyclopedia of the Bible,*
              Volume One, 845-857 Grand Rapids: Zondervan

Kittel, Gerhard &
Friderich, Gerhard, eds.
    1985   *Theological Dictionary of the New Testament: Abridged in One Volume*
              Grand Rapids: Eerdmans Publishing Co.

Knight, George W.
    1992   *Commentary on the Pastoral Epistles*
              New International Greek Testament Commentary
              Grand Rapids: Eerdmans Publishing Co.

Laney, J. Carl
    1985   *Guide to Church Discipline*
              Minneapolis: Bethany House Publishers

Lea, Thomas D. &
Griffin, Jr., Hayne P.
    1992   *1, 2 Timothy/Titus* The New American Commentary
              Nashville: Broadman Press

MacGorman, J.W.
    1991   "The Discipline of the Church," in *The People of God*, 74-84
              Nashville: Broadman Press

Machen, J. Gresham
    1994   *Christianity and Liberalism*
              Grand Rapids: Eerdmans Publishing Co. (reprint)

Morris, Leon
    1974   *The Gospel According to Luke*
              Grand Rapids: Eerdmans Publishing Co.

Morris, Leon
    1971   *The Epistles of Paul to the Thessalonians*
              Grand Rapids: Eerdmans Publishing Co.

Nelson, Alan E.
    1994   *Broken in the Right Place: How God Tames the Soul*
              Nashville: Thomas Nelson Publishers

Palmer, Donald C.
    1990   *Managing Conflict Creatively*
            Pasadena: William Carey Library

Ridderbos, Herman
    1977   *Paul: An Outline of His Theology*
            Grand Rapids: Eerdmans Publishing Co.

Rienecker, Fritz &
Rogers, Cleon
    1980   *Linguistic Key to the Greek New Testament*
            Grand Rapids: Regency Reference Library

Sande, Ken
    1992   *The Peacemaker*
            Grand Rapids: Baker Book House

Schaff, Philip ed.
    1983   *The Creeds of Christendom, Vol 3*
            Grand Rapids: Baker Books

Stott John
    1994   *Romans*
            Downers Grove: InterVarsity Press

Strauch, Alexander
    1988   *Biblical Eldership*
            Littleton: Lewis and Roth Publishers

Tasker, R.V.G.
    1976   *The General Epistle of James*
            Grand Rapids: Eerdmans Publishing Co.

Tidball, Derek J.
    1986   *Skillful Shepherds*
            Grand Rapids: Zondervan

Wallace, Ronald
    1974   "Discipline," in
            The New International Dictionary of the Christian Church 302
            Grand Rapids: Zondervan

White, John &
Blue, Ken
    1985   *Church Discipline that Heals*
            Downers Grove: InterVarsity Press

Zerwick, Max &
Grosvenor, Mary
    1974   *A Grammatical Analysis of the Greek New Testament Vols. 1&2*
            Rome: Biblical Institute Press